ESPN ULTIMATE NASCAR

100 DEFINING MOMENTS IN STOCK CAR RACING HISTORY

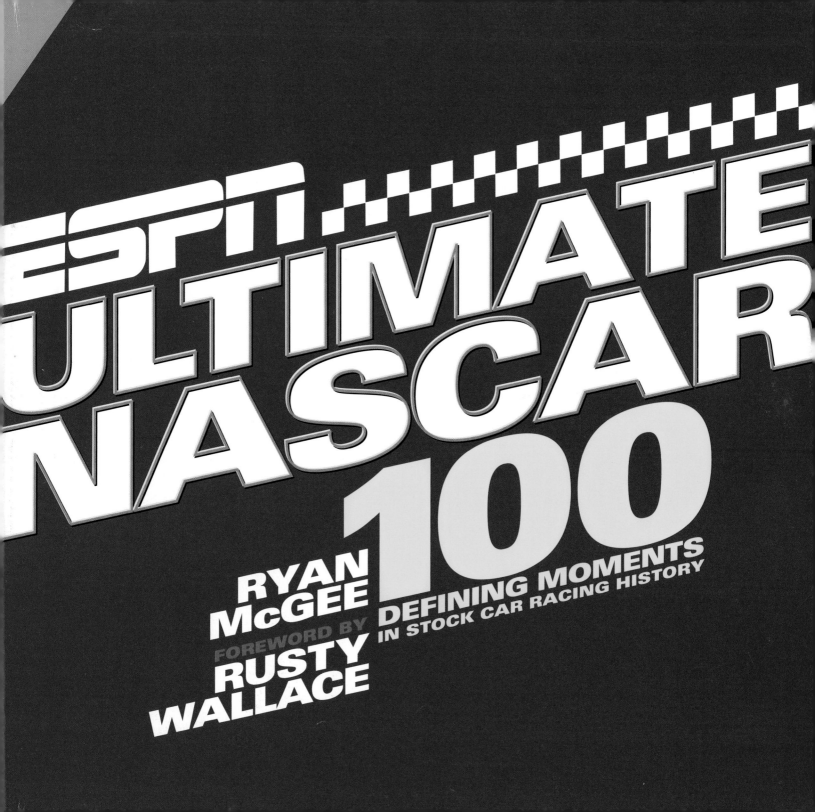

ESPn

ULTIMATE
NASCAR
100

RYAN McGEE

FOREWORD BY
RUSTY WALLACE

DEFINING MOMENTS
IN STOCK CAR RACING HISTORY

ISBN-13: 978-1-933060-25-5
ISBN-10: 1-933060-25-5

ESPN books are available for special promotions and premiums.
For details contact Michael Rentas, Assistant Director, Inventory Operations, Hyperion,
77 West 66th Street, 11th floor, New York, New York 10023, or call 212-456-0133.

FIRST EDITION

10 9 8 7 6 5 4 3 2 1

CONTENTS

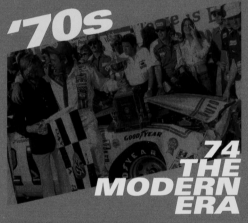

'90s

160
THE BREAK-THROUGH YEARS

FOREWORD LIFE IN THE FAST LANE
BY RUSTY WALLACE

Today I have a profound appreciation for the history of NASCAR. As a driver, I feel like you should never ever forget two things: where you came from and where NASCAR came from. But to be honest, I didn't always feel that way.

My career overlapped three of the greatest generations NASCAR has ever seen, from the guys who built the sport to the guys I came up with to finally, this young generation of today.

I ran my first Winston Cup race at Atlanta in 1980, and I remember looking out the window and being in total awe. Seeing guys like Bobby Allison and Cale Yarborough racing door-to-door with me—what a thrill! And when that red-and-blue No. 43 STP car of Richard Petty's went by me, I thought, How the hell did I get out here with these guys?

(Was it really a quarter of a century ago? I can close my eyes and see every detail just like it was yesterday.)

Then I made a common mistake for a young racer: I got cocky.

As those legends I was so in awe of got older and started slowing down a little, all I could think was that they were getting in my way, and I wasn't real nice about it. Then in the early 1990s, when I really had the most personal success, I grew out of that phase. Man, I am so glad that I did. I realized that being a NASCAR driver is a privilege and that getting to know the people who built this sport is just as big an honor.

During my last years behind the wheel, a new group of young guys showed up and started winning races. Most of them went out and made the same mistake I did, thinking they were the greatest drivers ever to come down the track and not caring about anything else, certainly not about those who had paved their way. But today, a lot of those same guys come up to me asking for advice, just like I eventually did with the guys who came before me.

Now my son, Steven, is on his way to becoming a Cup driver, and whenever I talk to him or anyone from his generation, I remind him to respect the sport. That means showing respect to the people who made NASCAR what it is today and taking the time to appreciate the history behind it.

That's why I'm excited about this book and about all the attention ESPN is giving to the history of NASCAR. Sometimes I feel like the people who built NASCAR get overlooked and forgotten, so anything we can do to give them their due, I am behind 100%.

ESPN put together a panel of NASCAR experts—sportswriters, historians, television commentators, even a few former drivers—and asked them to select their top 100 moments from a list of nominees. Those moments are presented here in chronological order, and the end result is pretty much a history of the sport's highlights.

I'm proud to say I took part in a lot of those moments, but at the time, you don't realize you're doing it. When you're racing, you aren't thinking about making history; you're just thinking about winning races and championships. But now it's nice to look back and realize that I had some part in creating some of the highlights that people consider to be among the ultimate in NASCAR history.

Now I look forward to being a part of the next 100 Defining Moments, only it won't be from behind the wheel but from inside the broadcast booth.

I can't wait.

—RUSTY WALLACE,
1989 NASCAR WINSTON CUP CHAMPION

'30s '40s & '50s

Florida, 1935: Daytona Beach was in trouble.

Long gone were the glamour-and-glitz days of the century's first two decades, when Rockefellers and Vanderbilts looked down from dune-top mansions to watch Fords and Stanley Steamers roar up the coast. Gone too were the land speed record-chasers, who had abandoned the hard-packed sands of Volusia County for the even faster salt flats of Utah.

When the racing cars left, so did Daytona Beach's tourists and their wallets. The elegant Hotel Ormond stood empty, and the restaurants around it were boarded up. Even more disturbing, the beach itself was quiet, the boom of V12 engines replaced only by lapping waves, rustling winds, and quarreling gulls.

Yes, Daytona Beach was in trouble in 1935, and nobody knew what to do. And yet, as civic leaders and local politicians and business owners hemmed and hawed over how to pull through, the man who would become their savior was quietly going about his business, fixing brakes and pumping gas just off the beach.

A DAY AT THE BEACH

During the winter of 1935, a local gas station owner named William Henry Getty France Sr.—everybody called him Big Bill— approached Daytona Beach's city council with a proposal for "stock" automobile races. The events would be held on a 1.6- mile beach-and-road course that on paper resembled a limp rubber band on a desktop. Long runs northward along the Atlantic coast and southward down the two-lane blacktop of Highway A1A would be punctu- ated by jarring turns on and off the beach.

A desperate city council agreed to the crazy scheme, despite protests from churches questioning the godliness of driving family cars at breakneck speeds on Sunday afternoons.

A $5,000 purse attracted 27 racers and 20,000 fans to the first race, which turned out to be an utter disaster.

Cars bogged down in soft sand on the turns. Fans bypassed ticket booths and marched over the dunes. An onrushing high tide forced an ending nine miles short of the scheduled 250. Canadian dirt-track ace Milt Marion earned $1,000 for the win; the city lost $22,000.

France, who finished fifth, was exhilarated by his brainchild's potential. He raced home to begin construction of another, much broader proposal.

Big Bill was dreaming big.

DECEMBER
14
1947

America was super-charged with optimism and enthusiasm after the great victory in World War II. Men and women had returned from Europe and the Pacific utterly unafraid of daring and intimately familiar with the capabilities of modern machinery. From Florida to California, Texas to Wisconsin, rural weekends pulsated with the hum of bored-out street engines, racing on home-plowed dirt ovals. Stock car racing was hot, but shady promoters and a confusing alphabet of sanctioning bodies threatened to keep it an underground phenomenon. Sensing a chance to seize power through planning, France corralled 35 racers and track owners from around the nation into the Ebony Room of the Streamline Hotel in Daytona Beach. At 1:00 p.m., the committee began to scribble on cocktail napkins as France declared, "Within our group rests the outcome of stock car racing in the country today. We have the opportunity to set it up on a big scale." The men talked, argued, and scribbled some more, and on the third day, they emerged with a name, the National Association of Stock Car Auto Racing, and a president, Bill France. Two months later, the new outfit was formally incorporated.

Time to go racing.

FEBRUARY 15, 1948
RED'S RUN

Robert "Red" Byron loved to race, even though it sometimes hurt.

During the late 1930s and early 1940s, Red tore up the Alabama dirt tracks until the Air Force tapped him to fly 58 missions over the Pacific as a tail gunner on a B-24. Then, in 1943, his plane was shot down over the Aleutians, and his left leg was mangled. Over the next two years, Red had so many reconstructive surgeries that some doctors suggested amputation.

But when NASCAR held its first official event at Daytona Beach in 1948, he was there. It wasn't easy. Car owner Ray Parks had to help wedge his driver behind the wheel of their Ford. Then he had to bolt the steel stirrup that encased Red's left foot and leg to the clutch.

After that, though, it was all Red.

The beach was packed with future NASCAR legends—Fireball Roberts, Fonty Flock, Marshall Teague—but Red paced the field. The win propelled him to the sport's first Modified championship. The following year, he won the Strictly Stock title.

Strictly Stock would come to be known as Grand National, then Winston Cup, and then Nextel Cup. But whatever the official title, the first name on the trophy will always be that of Red Byron, who chose speed over pain and found racing glory along the way.

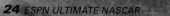

Rounding the turn in 1951, two years after NASCAR's first Strictly Stock event.

JUNE 19, 1949

DARING, DRAMA, DISBELIEF

Hard-core racers loved NASCAR's Modified division. The cars were loud, fast, and exotic. But France wanted fresh faces in the grandstand, not just gearheads and grease monkeys. He wanted moms and dads, kids and grandparents. And the way to woo everyday folks, he concluded, was with the cars they drove to the store, work, and school: Fords, Lincolns, Hudsons, Buicks.

On a balmy Sunday afternoon in West Charlotte, North Carolina, 33 such cars took the green flag for a 150-mile race billed by NASCAR as its first Strictly Stock event. Straight off the street with duct tape numbers slapped onto their doors, the familiar-looking rides were driven by moonshiners, lumberjacks, tobacco farmers, a milkman, even a housewife from Dahlonega, Georgia.

Ordinary folks, ordinary cars, but not so ordinary speeds.

The dirt oval was pocked with shoe-box-size potholes and jaw-busting bumps that cracked the sedans like walnuts. But local hero Glenn Dunnaway bounced smoothly over every obstacle. Too smoothly.

More than 13,000 fans watched Dunnaway's Ford cross the line first, but as the crowd filed home, the Gastonia, North Carolina, driver's win was stripped from him after an inspection revealed altered rear springs, common in liquor hauling but illegal in NASCAR. Kansan Jim Roper, who had finished three laps down, was declared the winner, despite weeks of protests and lawsuits by Dunnaway's team.

In just one day, NASCAR's new division had its first winner, first loser, and first controversy.

More important, it had its first headline in the sports pages.

FIELD OF DREAMS

Meet Harold Brasington, village idiot.

In 1933, the South Carolina gravel salesman attended the Indianapolis 500 and was so moved by the experience that he began to dream aloud about bringing big-time auto racing to his hometown, 690 miles to the southeast.

The good people of Darlington, South Carolina, were nice enough to listen to Brasington's grandiose plan but exploded into laughter whenever he left the room.

In a vision straight out of W.P. Kinsella's *Field of Dreams*, Brasington cranked up his bulldozer and sculpted a one-and-a-quarter-mile oval race track in a cotton field. Still, no one believed that anyone would come to the no-man's-land of Darlington County to run a stock car race, let alone pay money to watch one.

SEPTEMB

But on Labor Day weekend at the midcentury mark,
25,000 fans came to watch a jam-packed field—three cars wide, 25
rows deep, with 17 states represented—take the green flag in the first Southern 500. As the NASCAR regulars attacked the asphalt the way they would a dirt track,
Hollywood stuntman Johnny "Madman" Mantz eased his lightweight Plymouth onto the apron
and cruised at a pedestrian 75 mph on a single set of bulky truck tires. Against the high-banked
turns, teams popped so many tires that crews desperate for replacements went into the infield and
stripped wheels off fans' street rides.

After six and a half hours of racing, Mantz pulled into Victory Lane a full nine laps ahead of Fireball Roberts,
in second place. The Southern 500, the first stock car race ever held on a paved superspeedway, instantly
become NASCAR's signature event, and Darlington became a world-renowned racing destination.

Meet Harold Brasington, town genius.

THE FINAL LAP

In just a decade, NASCAR had grown from a dream on a napkin to a national powerhouse, with 51 races a year. But this would be the last visit to the actual beach at Daytona Beach, where it all started.

Michigan's Paul Goldsmith launched his Pontiac into a huge early lead. Then, with nine laps remaining, he got some company from Virginian Curtis Turner. But as Turner was setting up his move to take over the lead, a lapped car forced him into the edge of the surf and into a spin.

During the excitement, Goldsmith's No. 3 car lost use of its windshield wipers, rendering his forward view useless in the sand. Eyeballing his way through the driver's side window, Goldy powered up the beach for the final time … and completely missed the North Turn. Cranking into a 180° turn, he returned to the race only inches ahead of Turner. The pair raced nose-to-tail down Highway A1A, hitting a bump near the end that airlifted them toward the finish line.

Goldsmith won by a few feet.

As the two cars hit the beach one last time for a farewell lap, Turner pulled up alongside him. "Damn fine race!" he hollered. "That's how you close a place!"

FEBRUARY 23 1958

Beach Results

PLACE	DRIVER AND HOME:	TYPE CAR
	Paul Goldsmith, St. Clair Shores, Mich.	'58 Pontiac
1	Curtis Turner, Roanoke, Va.	'58 Ford
2	Jack Smith, Atlanta, Ga.	'58 Pontiac
3	Joe Weatherly, Norfolk, Va.	'58 Ford
4	Gwyn Staley, N. Wilkesboro, N.C.	'57 Chevrolet
5	Lee Petty, Randleman, N.C.	'57 Oldsmobile
6	Buck Baker, Spartanburg, S.C.	'58 Chevrolet
7	Eddie Pagan, Lynwood, Calif.	'57 Ford
8	Fireball Roberts, Daytona Beach, Fla.	'58 Buick
9	Cotton Owens, Spartanburg, S.C.	'57 Pontiac
10	Jimmy Thompson, Monroe, N.C.	'57 Pontiac
11	Dean Layfield, Wellsville, N.Y.	'58 Chevrolet
12	Bill Morton, Church Hill, Tenn.	'57 Ford
13	Marvin Panch, Charlotte, N.C.	'57 Ford
14	Charlie Stone, Austel, Ga.	'57 Chevrolet
15	Ward Towers, Cornith, N.Y.	'57 Ford
16	Lloyd Ragon, Syracuse, N.Y.	'57 Oldsmobile
17	Cecil Wray, Middletown, Ohio	'56 Chevrolet
18	Richard Foley, Montreal, Can	'58 Pontiac
19	Dick Dailey, Grove City, Pa.	'57 Chevrolet
20	Joe Lee Johnson, Chattanooga, Tenn.	'57 Ford
21	Carl Tyler, Bradford, Pa.	'56 Ford
22	Whitey Norman, Winston-Salem, N.C.	'56 Ford
23	Buzz Woodward, Coatsville, Pa.	'57 Ford
24	Eddie Skinner, Yerington, Nev.	'56 Chevrolet
25	L. D. Austin, Greenville, N.C.	'58 Ford
26	Phil Orr, Orlando, Fla.	'57 Pontiac
27	Bob Walden, High Point, N.C.	'57 Chevrolet
28	Frankie Schneider, Lambertville, N.J.	'57 Mercury
29	Billy Myers, Germanton, N.C.	'58 Plymouth
30	Johnny Allen, Fayetteville, N.C.	'58 Ford
31	Bobby Lee, Sumter, S.C.	'57 Mercury
32	Johnny Mackison, Delta, Pa.	'57 Ford
33	Kenny Love, Chicage Heights, Ill.	'57 Chevrolet
34	Brownie King, Johnson City, Tenn.	'58 Chevrolet
35	Banjo Mathews, Asheville, N.C.	'57 Ford
36	Bob Pronger, Chicago, Ill.	'58 Chevrolet
37	Rex White, Silver Spring, Md.	'57 Ford
38	Wilbur Rakestraw, Dallas, Ga.	'57 Chevrolet
39	Dariel Dieringer, Inianapolis, Ind.	'57 Chevrolet
40	Tiny Lund, Harlan, Iowa	'57 Ford
41	Bill Corley, Jackson, Miss.	'57 Dodge
	___, Orlando, Fla.	'57 Ford
	___, ___sbury, Pa.	'58 Pontiac

500 MILE INTERNATIONAL SWEEPSTAKES
AND OTHER RACING EVENTS
Feb. 20, 21, 22 - 1959

10th Annual
Safety and
Performance Trials
Feb. 15-19, 1959

PRICE $1.00

Daytona International Speedway
"WORLD'S FASTEST AND FINEST RACE COURSE"
DAYTONA BEACH, FLORIDA

FEB 22 1959

Bill France knew that for NASCAR to grow into a major league sport, it needed a major league venue. So once again he approached Daytona Beach city officials, this time with plans for a racetrack that would be "the world center of racing."

For 15 months, construction crews toiled in the muddy sand three miles inland from the old beach-and-road course. And on a sunny Sunday afternoon, 59 cars rolled onto the two-and-a-half-mile track for the

A GREAT AMERICAN RACE

first-ever Daytona 500.

Fans stood slack-jawed with disbelief for the entire 3-hour, 41-minute event. Anyone not staggered by the sheer speed was sent over the edge by the finish, when Lee Petty, Johnny Beauchamp, and the lapped car of Little Joe Weatherly crossed the finish line three wide at 140 mph. Both Petty and Beauchamp rolled to Victory Lane, where Beauchamp was declared the winner.

But Petty did what Petty did best—he filed a protest. For three days, France's team examined photographs as they trickled in from around the country. Finally, at 6:00 p.m. on February 25, thanks to film from Hearst Metrotone News of the Week, Petty was declared the winner by two feet and awarded the trophy quietly among a handful of friends and family. Among the proud kin was 21-year old son Richard, who had finished 57th in just his 11th NASCAR race.

Lee's next protest wouldn't leave Richard quite so happy.

FATHER KNOWS BEST

Richard Petty was going to be a race car driver. His DNA demanded it. Petty's 98-year-old great-grandfather had died while floor-boarding a Model T on a North Carolina back road. And father Lee was already a two-time NASCAR champion and winner of 41 races.

Forced by his dad to sit in the pits until he turned 21, Richard made his debut two weeks after blowing out the candles. In his first 16 tries, he earned four top 10s.

Richard reached his genetic destiny at Atlanta's Lakewood Speedway, where he took his first checkered flag. But the second-place finisher filed a protest to have the scoring charts reviewed and the laps recounted.

Who was that sore loser? Daddy.

"People were like, 'I can't believe that he'd do that!' " Richard recalled nearly half a century later. "And I said, 'Then you never met Lee Petty.' "

Turns out father did know best. The original outcome was overturned, and Lee Petty was declared the winner. So instead of celebrating the No. 43 car's first win, the Petty family assembled to congratulate the driver of the No. 42 car on win No. 42.

Richard's first victory came eight months later in Charlotte, this time with Lee safely behind the wall with burned-up spark plugs.

JUNE 14, 1959

'60S

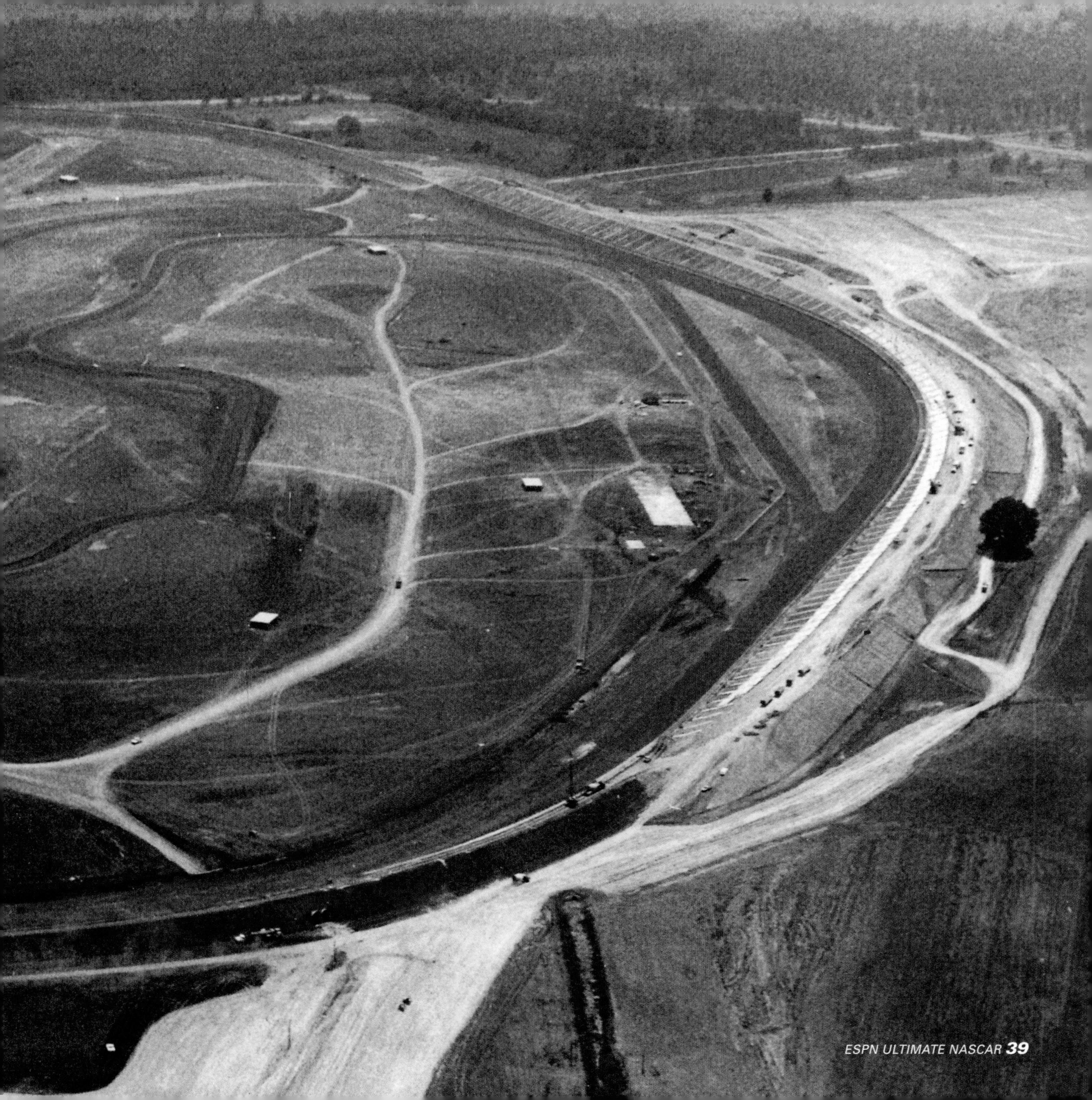

NASCAR entered its second decade riding earthmovers and backhoes. The spine of the sport (not to mention its soul) remained dirt tracks, but promoters were anxious to cash in on the success of the big blacktop circuits in Darlington and Daytona.

By 1960, the one-and-a-half-mile Charlotte Motor Speedway and the Atlanta International Raceway had opened in the South, and the sparkling Marchbanks Speedway had been christened in California. Entrepreneurs from around the country descended upon Daytona, hoping to convince France to construct racetracks in their hometowns. Meanwhile, France was dreaming of a Daytona sister track in rural Alabama.

NASCAR's speedway era was under way. But with speed comes danger, and the racetrack revolution would force a safety evolution.

"YOU ARE WATCHLIN

CBS Sports broadcaster Bud Palmer had seen it all—and done a bunch of it. Born in Hollywood, the son of an actor, Palmer played forward at Princeton, where he was one of the pioneers of the jump shot. Later, after playing for the New York Knicks, Palmer went into sports broadcasting. He hosted *Jackpot Bowling Starring Milton Berle*. He covered the Masters, the NBA Finals, and the Olympics for CBS Sports. At 40, Palmer was one of the top play-by-play guys in the business.

But this—this was something different. For the first-ever live telecast of a NASCAR event, CBS shipped a crew of 50 technicians and several truckloads of cameras to Daytona for a special edition of *CBS*

CHING
VE....

Sports Spectacular. Palmer, 6'4", hunched down over a TV monitor, squinted through the Florida sun and provided an historic vroom!-by-vroom! account of a major event in a sport he knew virtually nothing about.

(Hey, he wasn't the only one. But that would soon change.)

For two hours, NASCAR was beamed into homes coast to coast. An estimated 17 million people tuned in to watch Daytona 500 qualifying races and two exhibitions on the infield road course.

They saw the future of stock car racing, and they liked it.

Two weeks later, NBC televised a four-lap sprint on its *Today* show, and ABC began searching for its own TV-friendly event.

Palmer said later he thought to himself at the time, We just might be on to something here.

FEBRUARY 14

ANYBODY FEEL A DRAFT?

The Chevy that Junior Johnson took to the 1960 Daytona 500 was dog slow, maybe 30 mph slower than the Pontiacs he'd be racing against. Junior knew it. His fellow drivers knew it. The fact that one of Johnson's sponsors was the owner of the Daytona Beach Kennel Club added a touch of unintended irony to his dilemma.

But then, purely by accident, Johnson discovered something that would transform NASCAR racing.

"Cotton Owens was on the pole," Johnson recalls. "In practice, I got right in on his rear bumper, and damn if I didn't stay right there. Everybody said, 'Man, you got that car up to speed!' What they didn't know was that I had discovered the aerodynamic draft."

During the race itself, Johnson spent four hours riding in the slipstream of the Pontiacs. With 10 laps to go, the back window suddenly popped out of race leader Bobby Johns' car, and the resulting vacuum sent Johns into a spin. Johnson coolly slid by into the lead and on to the win, the most startling victory of his Paul Bunyanesque life.

"We ran about 150 miles an hour at Daytona," the former moonshine runner says with a smile. "Hell, I'd run cars faster than that on the highway."

1960

FEBRUARY 24 1963

WIN ONE FOR THE-- MARVIN?

Glen and Leonard Wood knew it was bad before anyone told them. They could see the trail of black smoke snaking up from between Turns 3 and 4. Their driver, Marvin Panch, was testing a Maserati for an upcoming sports car race when it went airborne, flipped, and caught fire. DeWayne "Tiny" Lund, a hulking but hard-luck racer who had traveled to Daytona just hoping for a ride in the 1963 Daytona 500, was coming through the infield tunnel when he saw the crash. He jumped the wall, dived into the flames, and dragged Panch free.

Hours later, Panch—taking on the role of George Gipp—looked up at the Wood brothers from his hospital bed and asked them to put Lund in his car for the race. They agreed to do so.

On race day, the crafty brothers employed one fewer pit stop than their competition by running the entire race on one set of tires and squeezing every last drop out of their gas tank. It worked. Lund outlasted Freddy Lorenzen, whose Ford choked out of fuel as it crossed the finish line.

A life saved. A career resurrected. A race won.

DECEMBER 1, 1963

CAPTURING THE FLAG

By the time Wendell Scott rolled into the Jacksonville Speedway Park for the Grand National, he had learned to squeeze a dollar as far as it would go. He'd built his car himself. He'd taught his two sons how to be a full-fledged pit crew. And he'd shown his entire family how to tune out the endless string of abuse and racial epithets that poured out of the grandstand at just about every track he visited on the NASCAR circuit.

"I already knew I was black," he explained in a 1985 interview. "NASCAR fans obviously knew I was black. But there were always a few folks kind enough to point it out anyway."

With 14 laps to go in the race, Scott motored his No. 34 Chevy around Richard Petty and into the lead. He crossed the finish line on Lap 200 but didn't see the checkered flag. So he ran another lap. No flag. One more lap. No flag.

Buck Baker was flagged the winner, triggering protests from both ends of Pit Road. After four hours of discussion, Scott was declared the winner by a full two laps over Baker. The crowd of 5,000 was long gone.

"Everybody there knew I had won," Scott said. "But the promoters didn't want to see what might happen if I was out there kissing beauty queens and accepting awards."

Four decades later, we know exactly what did happen: Wendell Scott became more than black or white.

Wendell Scott became a winner.

CHAMPION KILLED—A head-on crash into a steel barrier rail on the No. 6 turn of the Riverside, Cal., road course cost the life of Grand National Champion Joe Weatherly on Jan. 19. Apparently, he died instantly of a crushed skull.

Weatherly, 41, one of the greatest champions in racing history, was on his 87th lap at the time, about 20 laps behind the leaders. Earlier in the 500-mile race, he had lost much time—maybe 40 or more minutes—while the transmission was changed in his '64 Mercury. He had just come out of a series of S-turns and was entering No. 6 turn when the accident occurred. No. 6 turns sharply to the right and is on a hill.

There is speculation that Joe's engine blew. When he hit the brakes, there were no brakes. Apparently, a piece from the engine had cut the brake line. Also, it is believed Weatherly's head hit the front roll bar. His helmet was not broken.

Weatherly won the grand national championship in 1962 and again in 1963. Fans voted him NASCAR's most popular driver in 1961, an honor he deeply appreciated. In 1953 he was NASCAR's National Modified champion. Funeral services were held in Norfolk, Va., his home town.

The last time a driver was killed in Grand National competition was Sept. 2, 1957, when Bobby Myers was fatally injured in the Southern 500 at Darlington. Since then, up to the Riverside race but not including it, all drivers had raced an aggregate of 1,092,576.5 miles in Grand National competition without a driver fatality.

JANUARY 19, 1964
FAREWELL, LITTLE JOE

Little Joe Weatherly was a certifiable wild man. He wrecked rental cars. He flew planes without navigational aids, choosing to "eyeball the road below." He stole competitors' car keys. And he spiked their water bottles, leaving them to wonder why they sometimes felt lightheaded so early during races.

Little Joe also won races. Lots of them. He piled up wins in NASCAR Modifieds and Convertibles, and in only 230 Grand National starts, the Clown Prince of Racing racked up 25 victories and won back-to-back titles in 1962 and 1963.

No matter what Weatherly raced, he refused to wear a shoulder harness, going lap belt only because, he explained, "I am not getting stuck in a fire." Besides, he added, "I like to flap around."

But when he lost his brakes on the road course at Riverside International Raceway in Riverside, California, at the Motor Trend 500, there was nothing to prevent his body from flying into the windshield, nothing to keep his helmet from colliding with the concrete wall, and in the end, nothing to save his life.

By season's end, a devastated NASCAR had mandated the use of shoulder belts and had begun to develop netting for driver-side windows.

Unfortunately, those would not be the last safety projects they would be forced to undertake in the 1964 season.

UNLEASHING THE BEAST

For two years, the NASCAR garage was filled with whispers about a monster in the works, an engine being created for Richard Petty that was so powerful and so advanced that Chrysler was keeping its development under wraps.

As Petty ran the first five races of 1964 with a year-old power plant, the top-secret beast was being put through its final paces on a test track somewhere deep in Texas. Then, when the Petty team arrived for the 1964 Daytona 500, they finally received their new engine: a monster 426-cubic-inch V-8 gorilla with hemispherical heads.

The Hemi had been born.

When unleashed, the No. 43 Plymouth became a guided missile, leading 184 of 200 laps and pulling Petty to his first Daytona 500 victory by more than a lap. "I wasn't exactly enjoying myself out there," Petty told reporters afterward in Victory Lane. "You start getting up to 170, and the car lets you know it."

As Ford and Chevy scrambled back to the drawing board, NASCAR started getting used to the newest entry in its driver-written dictionary: "Bad fast."

FEB-23,1964

MAY 24 1964

In the mid-1960s, Glenn Roberts was NASCAR's biggest star, with a photogenic family, 33 wins under his belt, and boy, what a nickname: Fireball!

As the World 600 hit Lap 7 at the Charlotte Motor Speedway, Fireball's trademark purple Ford was settling into its rhythm. Then Junior Johnson's Chevy clipped Ned Jarrett's Ford. >>>

"MY GOD, NED! HELP ME! I'M ON FIRE!"

>>> Roberts spun his car to avoid the wreck but hit a gate opening along the wall. In one horrifying instant, his car flipped, the fuel tank ripped, and an explosion rocked the backstretch.

Jarrett ran to his friend's aid and found him hanging upside down: "My God, Ned! Help me! I'm on fire!" His own hands burning, Jarrett cut Roberts loose and tore off his clothes, preserving the 20% of his body not already burned.

Six weeks later, NASCAR rolled into Roberts' hometown of Daytona for the Firecracker 400 when word reached the garage: Fireball Roberts was dead.

They held the race, then everybody traveled across town to the funeral to say goodbye.

If the death of a friend and a colleague can have a benefit, it is this: NASCAR moved swiftly to introduce rubber fuel cells that are nearly impossible to puncture and which have since saved countless lives.

That is Fireball Roberts' legacy.

WELCOME HOME, POPS Curtis "Pops" Turner was the loudest man in America's loudest sport. Pops threw the rowdiest parties, ran with the wildest women, and pushed his cars into places they simply weren't supposed to go. But for nearly half a decade, Turner went silent, banished from the league he'd helped build.

In 1961, Turner needed financing to bail out his struggling Charlotte Motor Speedway. Along came Jimmy Hoffa, who offered to provide that funding—if Turner created a Teamsters-backed drivers union. Bill France hated unions, feared Hoffa's "friends," and was spooked by the thought of

JULY 31, 1965

organized gambling at NASCAR events. So he crushed the deal and shackled Turner with a lifetime ban from racing.

As it turned out, "lifetime" meant 239 races.

In the summer of 1965, faced with dipping attendance, the deaths of Roberts and Weatherly, and a fight with Chrysler over the legality of the Hemi, Big Bill called Pops Turner and invited him back into the garage.

Two weeks later, Turner rolled onto the track in an attempt to qualify for a 200-lapper in Spartanburg, South Carolina—and promptly crashed into the first-turn wall. The result was a wild standing ovation from a sellout crowd. They weren't cheering the wreck, of course; they were cheering Pops Turner's return.

And cheering loudly, befitting the man.

GENTLEMAN NED'S JAUNT

SEPTEMBER 1965

In a wild world of speed-crazy, hell-raising rowdies, Ned Jarrett was a soft-spoken, Sunday school-teaching family man. He ran his own race team and preached about the duties of being a role model. He provided financial support for cash-strapped racers like Wendell Scott and took rookies under his wing. Gentleman Ned.

But when the green flag dropped, there was nothing gentle about Gentleman Ned. By Labor Day of 1965, Jarrett had already won a NASCAR championship and was sitting on 48 career wins.

On a stifling day at the Southern 500 in Darlington, in a Ford that was threatening to cook itself, a flu-fevered Jarrett smoked the field. He grabbed the lead with 39 laps to go, and by the time he crossed the finish line, his 14-lap margin of victory was the largest gap in NASCAR history.

Eight weeks later, Jarrett ended the season with his 50th career win, his second NASCAR title—and a broad hint that retirement was imminent. (He ran 21 races in 1966, then made it official.)

An exit worthy of a gentleman.

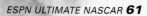

OCTOBER

TURNER MAKES THE TURN

Pops Turner's return hadn't been the in-your-face comeback success story he had hoped for. Back from his "lifetime" ban, he couldn't convince his old friends at Ford that there was still some winning left in his alcohol-preserved, 41-year-old bones.

After crashing during qualifying at Spartanburg his first time back, Turner pulled off after 51 laps at Darlington and was rel-egated to Junior Johnson's backup car at Hickory and Richmond. Then, finally, Ford called and put Pops in a second Wood Brothers ride for four races.

The seventh leg of his comeback was in the American 500, the first race at Harold Brasington's newest creation, the North Carolina Speedway in Rockingham. After five hours of racing and one violent slap of the wall, the old man found himself standing in Victory Lane for the first time in six years—and what would be the last time in his career.

Exhausted from holding off youngster Cale Yarborough and exhilarated by the cheers that rained down from the fans, Turner told the local newspaper, "I feel like a man who just got out of jail."

FEB

SUPER

26

MARIO

1967

It didn't make sense when Ford told team owners John Holman and Ralph Moody to put some Italian kid in their race car. Mario Andretti was too small. He was used to those lighter, open-wheel cars. He'd never run 'shine or stuffed his jaw with chaw. Did he even speak English? But when the green flag dropped at the ninth Daytona 500, he was too far out in front for any of that to matter.

"No one ran up high back then," Moody recalled 20 years later. "But he stayed up there all day long. Ran out of gas, coasted in, ran everybody down again—twice. Tell me he can't drive a damn race car."

The King meets the press in 1968.

OCTOBER 1, 1967
LONG LIVE THE KING

Richard Petty needed a nickname. In a garage filled with guys named Fuzzy, Axle, Tiny, and Spook, Petty was just plain Richard. The media tried Rapid Richard, even Dick, but nothing stuck.

Then came the summer of 1967. Earlier in the season, Petty had broken his father's career-wins record of 54, but what Just Plain Richard Petty did during the season's second half was nothing less than mount the most dominant run in the history of American motorsports.

From July 9 through October 1, he won 15 of 18 races, including 10 in a row from mid-August forward, finishing up at the North Wilkesboro Speedway in the Wilkes 400. During those 10 races, he started from the pole six times and led 1,781 of the 2,931 total laps run. Little brother Maurice and cousin Dale Inman set up the Plymouth Belvedere, and Petty drove the living hell out of it. Everybody worked, everybody won. In a 48-race season, the No. 43 car finished first 27 times, second seven times, and cruised to its second Grand National championship.

Somewhere in the middle of it all, an appropriate nickname finally emerged. Turns out it was easy. A man so untouchable yet so revered could carry only one title.

The King.

THE RAPID RISE AND FASTER FALL OF A TRIPLE CROWN WINNER

"You could stuff his brains into your watch pocket," a rival said of LeeRoy Yarborough, "but you couldn't fit all his courage into a dump truck."

A stocky racer in the Modified division from Jacksonville, Yarbrough sported pork chop sideburns and a Frankie Avalon pompadour that framed wild, darting eyes. His driving style was even more outrageous, with a devil-may-care fearlessness that reminded Junior Johnson of no other race car driver since, well, Junior Johnson.

Behind the wheel of Johnson's Ford in 1969, Yarborough won the Daytona 500, the World 600, and, on a windy, rainy South Carolina day at the Darlington Raceway, the Southern 500.

That made LeeRoy Yarborough NASCAR's first Triple Crown winner. But as quickly as he had arrived, he also vanished. Two hard hits in 1970 and 1971 quickened a downfall started by a secret addiction to painkillers. In February 1980, he was arrested for strangling his mother at their Jacksonville home. (She survived the attack; he was later acquitted by reason of insanity.)

In 1984, after years of psychiatric treatment, paid for mostly by Junior Johnson, LeeRoy Yarborough died in a Florida state hospital at the age of 46.

9-13-69 #9

SEPTEMBER 14, 1969

THE STARS

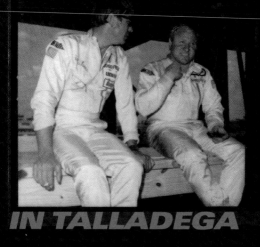

GO OUT IN TALLADEGA

The Alabama International Motor Speedway in Talladega was supposed to be a sister to Daytona. In fact, it was Daytona on steroids: 2.66 miles with six-story turns banked 33°. When NASCAR teams arrived for the inaugural event, the Talladega 500, everyone expected a whole mess of speed. What they hadn't predicted was a week of shredded tires and fractured friendships.

As practice speeds came within a hair of 200 mph, tires self-destructed after only two laps and tempers followed. Meetings broke out in every corner of the garage, with voices rising among drivers, tire technicians, team owners, and NASCAR officials. Led by Richard Petty, 37 competitors told Bill France that the race should be postponed until the tires caught up with the cars. France, sensing the makings of another push for a drivers union, responded with characteristic bluntness: "There will be a race tomorrow, but if you want to go home, then go."

And so they did. That left a Sunday field formed by 36 relative unknowns, many

>>>

of them recruited by France on Saturday evening. They ran the 500 miles but stopped under caution every 25 laps to check and change tires. Richard Brickhouse earned the win—the only one of his career—and a check for $25,000.

Seven months later, the stars returned to Talladega to race, with nary a complaint among them.

Rack up another win for Big Bill France.

"THERE WILL BE A RACE TOMORROW

BUT IF YOU WANT **TO GO HOME,** **THEN GO!"**

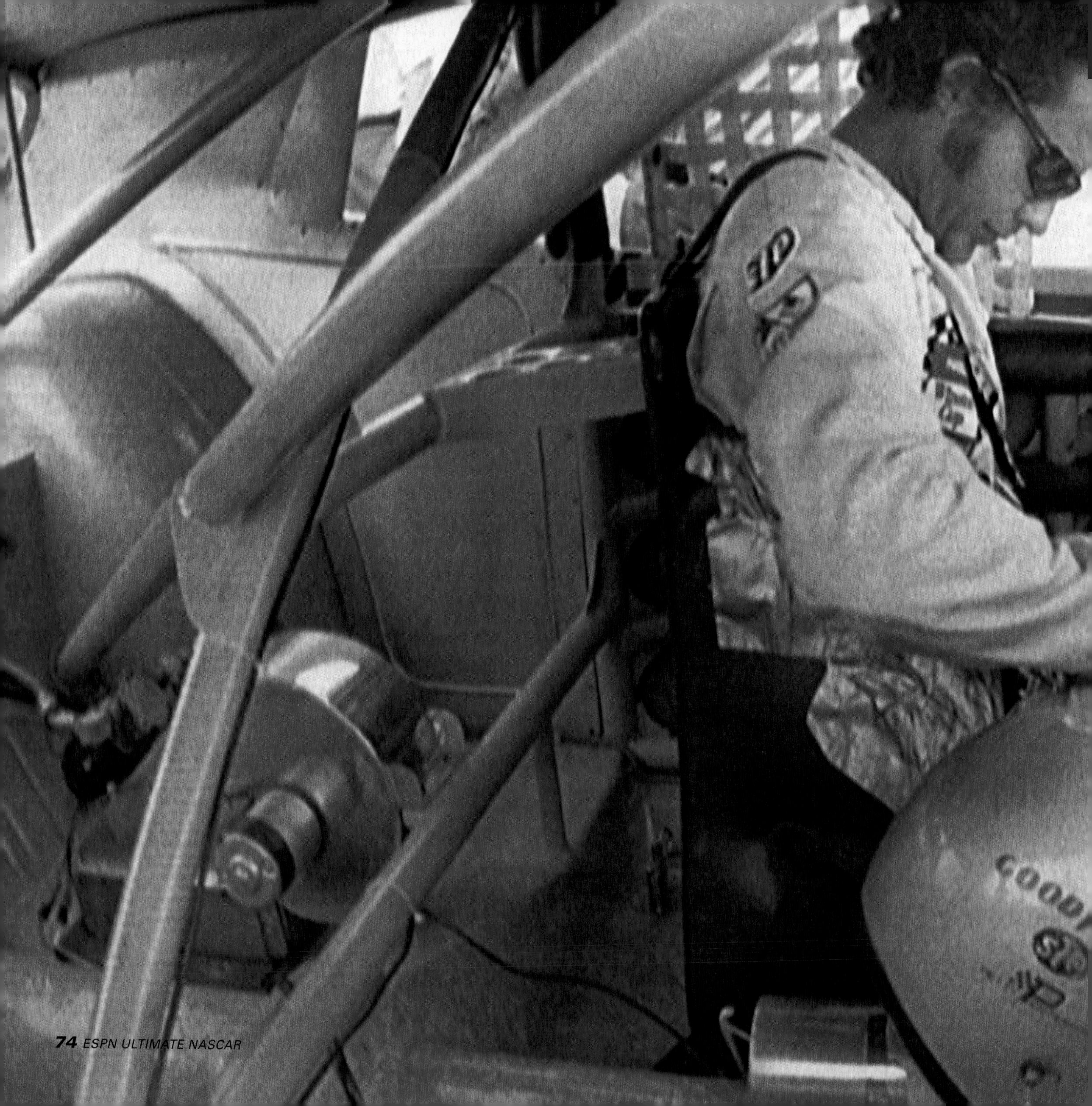

'70s

Despite hammer-down growth in its first quarter-century, NASCAR had about the same core fan base in 1970 as it had in 1948.

Bill France was still in charge. The cars were still reasonable facsimiles of their carport counterparts. And most outfits within the sport still operated at a deficit, with budget ledgers covered in red ink and racing machines covered in red clay dust from Southeastern dirt tracks.

But by the time the 1970s ended, so had the hardscrabble existence of the poor-but-proud participants, thanks to an odd mixture of radio, television, cigarettes, and asphalt.

The final ingredient in NASCAR's huge status leap from regional diversion to major sport was nothing less than the greatest rivalry in the history of American motorsports. Richard Petty vs. David Pearson was North Carolina vs. South Carolina, media darling vs. recluse, Chrysler vs. Mercury.

Or, to put in simpler terms ... The King vs. the Silver Fox.

DON'T TOUCH THAT DIAL
FEBRUARY 22, 1970

Auto racing on the radio? You gotta be kidding. On the *radio*? Who's going to listen?

Bill France knew exactly who. He knew that his NASCAR fans were car people, and he knew that when they couldn't get to the race on Sunday, they'd likely be out driving around in their own vehicles, and, yes, he knew they'd be listening to their car radios the whole time.

TV, on the other hand, scared France. Why would people pay for tickets to go to a race if they could sit on their couches at home and watch it for free?

But radio, if done right, with a knowledgeable voice describing the action to a backdrop of Vroom! Vroom! Vroom! would be the perfect tease.

Radio helped make baseball the national

(as opposed to a merely local) pastime. Why couldn't it do the same for racing?

Daytona's WNDB-AM had already broadcast a few races, and France found a perfect broadcaster in New England storyteller Ken Squier, who had a voice as thick as Vermont maple syrup. The two joined up at the 1970 Daytona 500, leveraging NASCAR's signature race and, later, the new track at Talladega to recruit 400 affiliates for MRN, the Motor Racing Network.

"People tuned in for the racing," Squier recalls, "but they ended up meeting personalities. We used taped interviews to establish these amazing racers as people. The listeners really connected."

As did the sport itself, which was soon racing coast to coast at the speed of sound.

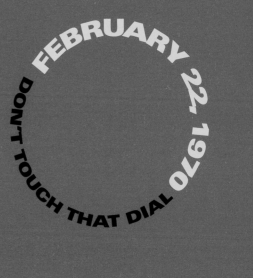

FEBRUARY 22, 1970

DON'T TOUCH THAT DIAL

MR. 200 MPH

Charger

Elzie Wylie Baker Jr. liked to go fast. Really fast. His father, Buck, won two NASCAR titles and 46 races, nearly all of which came on the tight, calculating short tracks. But Buddy was all about superspeedways.

"That boy just wants to go as fast as possible," his father once said. "The faster he goes, the better he is. He'd draft off a damn hot dog wrapper if it meant picking up speed."

So when Chrysler's management team decided to take a shot at cracking the 200 mph barrier, they placed a call to Baker and his Cotton Owens-prepared No. 6 Dodge Daytona. How fast can you say "Yes!"? And so, on a cool Alabama spring morning, with no one in attendance but a few Detroit suits and NASCAR brass, Baker's winged machine took to the high banks of the Talladega Superspeedway.

By the third lap, Baker was in the wind. As he hit the line, he looked left to the number on the infield scoreboard: 200.447 mph, a world record for a single lap on a closed course.

"I could have gone 210," Baker says today. "But Mr. 200 Miles Per Hour has a nice, round ring to it."

If Junior Johnson learned only one lesson during a lifetime of racing, it was this: Money = Speed. With this thought in mind, the NASCAR legend drove into Winston-Salem in late 1970 to chat up the deep-pockets people of the R.J. Reynolds Tobacco Company.

Big Tobacco was smarting from a government-issued ban on television advertising, and RJR was more than ready to hear Johnson's car-sponsorship pitch. After all, racing fans were smokers, and Junior Johnson was just about the most popular racer at the track.

But as the conversation shifted into high gear, both parties suddenly realized the potential for a much larger opportunity, and the talk ended with Johnson's pushing Bill France's phone number across the desk.

When NASCAR's top series hit the track for the 1971 season, the Grand National division had become the NASCAR Winston Cup Series. RJR posted $100,000 in year-end bonus money and in return bypassed the ad ban by plastering its rich, red logo on racetracks, race cars, and sports pages across the country.

Cigarettes and gasoline: an explosive combination that forever changed a sport.

VIVE LES FRANCES!

For a quarter of a century, as the founder and one-and-only president of NASCAR, Big Bill France had beaten back rival leagues, driver revolts, and Jimmy Hoffa.

But not even Big Bill could figure out how to beat back Father Time, and his pedal-to-the-metal sport needed a younger leader who could stay out in front.

And so, at the start of NASCAR's 25th season, a new France crawled in behind the wheel—William Clifton France Jr., better known to everybody in racing as Bill Junior.

Bill Junior swept into office on a wave of change. The schedule was trimmed from 48 races to 31. Any race of fewer than 250 miles was lopped off. And all races were moved to the weekend so as to command maximum exposure. The sport, with Detroit factory support drying up, was at an obvious transition point.

But what to call this new age?

"Write it down," Bill Junior told a gathering of reporters at the start of the 1972 season. "We're going to call it NASCAR's Modern Era."

Big Bill and Bill Junior, c. 1956.

"If A.J. Foyt wasn't for real," a rival once said, "we'd have to make him up."

Anthony Joseph Foyt Jr. was—is—the greatest, most versatile racer ever born within the borders of the United States. Anyone who doubts that can ask A.J. himself. By 1972, Foyt had already won three Indianapolis 500s, five IndyCar championships, the 24 Hours of LeMans, and so many sprint car events that he lost count.

But Foyt's annual trip to the Daytona 500, NASCAR's biggest event, always seemed to end with one of his legendary Texas tantrums. In 1971, Foyt was en route to victory

FEBRUARY 20, 1972
SUPER TEX BEATS THE HEX

when a twisted fuel line choked his engine dry, leading to cries of sabotage from car owners Glen and Leonard Wood.

One year later, Super Tex left nothing to chance when he finally won on his ninth trip to the beach. Foyt's No. 21 Mercury led the final 300 miles and won by nearly three miles over second-place finisher Charlie Glotzbach.

"There's a lot of us glad A.J. doesn't come down here full-time," Richard Petty said to reporters after the race. "There might not be any races left for us to win."

A.J. Foyt and his ride of preference, c. 1958.

HOME COOKIN'

OCTOBER 21, 1973 Somehow, Benny Parsons and L.G. DeWitt kept up. Every week, they loaded up their sponsorless race car in tiny Ellerbe, North Carolina, and headed off to places like Brooklyn (the one in Michigan), College Station (in Texas), and Riverside (in California). The big guys always won, but Benny and L.G. punched out top-10s like a couple of telegraph operators.

When the Ellerbe Gang arrived for the season-ending American 500 at DeWitt's North Carolina Speedway in Rockingham, they held a slim points lead over Cale Yarborough. Only 15 minutes from home, they were the crowd favorite. But on Lap 13, the stands went silent as the No. 72 car spun out helplessly, its right side sheered away—sheet metal, roll bars, everything. Parsons

sat exposed, stunned, and resigned to losing the title.

Suddenly, other crews began cannibalizing their own cars and bringing over parts. For over an hour, they hammered and welded, busting a gut to get the Ellerbe Gang back in the race. Maybe it was because they wanted the little guy to win for a change. Perhaps they just liked Parsons and DeWitt. Whatever the reason, a crew of dozens from as many different crews got BP back on the track. He finished 184 laps behind Yarborough, but 67 points ahead in the race for the championship.

As they had done all season, Benny Parsons and L.G. DeWitt packed their things, loaded up the car, and headed back to Ellerbe. But not until they had shaken every hand in the garage and waved to every single fan all the way home.

(UN)FRIENDLY RIVALRY

One lap to go. David Pearson led the 1974 Firecracker 400, with archrival Richard Petty on his rear deck lid. All 65,000 fans in attendance knew what was coming next. So did Pearson: Petty would wait until the two cars hit the backstretch, then slingshot his No. 43 Dodge into the lead.

Only Petty never got the chance.

Pearson's car suddenly lurched, slowed, and dove to the inside apron as Petty swept into the lead. The crowd gasped and broadcaster Keith Jackson stumbled over his words trying to describe what he (and everyone else) surmised must have been a crushing mechanical failure.

But the Silver Fox wasn't dead. He was just hibernating.

As Petty ran along the backstretch, his rearview mirror was suddenly filled with the unmistakable white hood of the clearly not-broken No. 21 Mercury, and at the finish line it was Pearson who managed to slingshot his way into Victory Lane.

The move was fearless, cunning, and unprecedented. To Petty, it was also reckless and unsafe, an opinion he later shared with anyone who would listen, including Pearson.

Petty-Pearson was already the biggest rivalry in the sport, but their head-to-heads had always been based on mutual respect and a two-decade friendship.

Now it was powered by something new: anger.

BENNY'S BIG DAY

FEBRUARY 16, 1975

The season after winning the championship, Benny Parsons struggled so badly that he approached L.G. DeWitt to turn in his resignation. L.G. persuaded him to give it one more season, but the new year started no better, with a bum oil pump at Riverside and a poor showing in Daytona 500 qualifying.

But as the 500 rolled on, the race came back to Benny. With 10 laps remaining and over half the 40 starters having dropped out of the race, Parsons ran a comfortable second, more than five seconds behind David Pearson.

"That's when the 43 car came out in front of me," Parsons recalls. Richard Petty had the fastest car that day but ran eight laps down with a cracked radiator. "He started motioning with his right hand, like, 'If you want to catch Pearson, come on.' "

Using the draft, Parsons let The King tow him to within one second of Pearson. Then, with two laps remaining, Pearson swerved to avoid a slower car and spun helplessly into the infield grass.

Said Parsons later: "I watched David spinning and thought to myself, BP, you just won yourself the Daytona 500!"

But even more important, at least to Richard Petty, David Pearson didn't.

5

PEARSON IN THE CLUTCH

Richard Petty and David Pearson raced against each other 550 times. The score: Petty 289-Pearson 261. In 63 of those races they finished 1-2: Pearson 33-Petty 30. They ranked 1-2 in wins, poles, and grandstand fights initiated.

At the 1976 Daytona 500, they were locked up again. On the final lap, Pearson led, with Petty in his slipstream. As they hit Turn 3, the STP Dodge flung alongside the Purolator Mercury, muscling into the lead as they rolled off Turn 4. "Then we hit with a bang," Pearson remembers, "and we got to spinning."

Spinning directly toward the finish line, Petty nearly won backward, but both cars slid into the infield lawn about 100 feet shy of the checkers. Through a cloud of tire smoke, fans saw The King trying to refire his stalled engine, when suddenly the Silver Fox emerged from the billow, bumper plowing grass.

Amid the chaos of the crash, Pearson had calmly stood on the clutch, keeping his engine running. Now he was going to win the Daytona 500, running all of 20 miles per hour.

In Victory Lane, Petty shook Pearson's hand: "Sorry about that, David."

"That's okay, Richard," Pearson said. "I know it wasn't on purpose. Besides, it turned out all right."

"Yeah ... for you."

FULL NAME Ralph (Dale) Earnhardt   NICKNAME _____
   (First) (Middle) (Last)

HOME ADDRESS: Street or Box _Sedan St_   State _NC_ Zip _28081_ Telephone (Area) (Number)

City _Kannapolis_   Present Age _23_ Height _6'_ Weight _165_

Birthdate _April 29, 51_
   (Month, Day, Year)

OCCUPATION (OTHER THAN RACING) _None_

MARRIED/SINGLE _Married_   WIFE'S NAME _Brenda_

CHILDREN (Names & Ages) _Kerry Dale, 5 / Kelly King 2 / Dale Junor 3 months_

PARENT'S NAMES: _Mrs. Ralph Lee Earnhardt - Martha_   LOCATION _Kannapolis_

SCHOOL ATTENDED: _A.L. Brown_

YEARS _10_ PARTICIPATED IN (sports) _Wrestling_   LOCATION _____

COLLEGE ATTENDED: _None_

YEARS ____ PARTICIPATED IN (sports) _____

CHURCH AFFILIATION _Lutheran_

ARMED SERVICES RECORD: YEARS ____ RANK ____

BRANCH _None_

HOBBIES _Hunting_

STARTED RACING (YEAR) _4_ TYPE RACING _Dirt, Out law Semi Modified_

FIRST RACE _Charlotte, Summer of 71, Semi Modified_ _Concord_ _7-29-73_
   (when, where, type)

WHAT HAPPENED IN FIRST RACE _Finish 10th_

ANY RACING TITLES _Won Semi Modified Point Champion at Chance lot_
   (what, where, when)

GREATEST RACING THRILL _When I won my first race at Chance lot in 74_

AMBITION (OTHER THAN RACING) _None_

SUPERSTITUTIONS _Green & peanuts_

TYPE CAR DRIVEN IN 1974 _1964 Chevelle_ WHAT CLASS RACING DO YOU INTEND TO FOLLOW IN 1975? _Sports man_

WHO IS YOUR FAVORITE AMONG PRESENT DRIVERS? _Bobby Isaac & Richard Petty_

ANY ADDITIONAL INFORMATION BELOW:

INCLUDE HEAD AND SHOULDER PICTURE OF YOURSELF. IF YOU DO NOT HAVE ONE AVAILABLE, DO YOU HAVE NAME AND ADDRESS OF PHOTOGRAPHER WHO WOULD HAVE SAME?

PHOTOGRAPHER _____   STREET _____

CITY _____   STATE ____ ZIP ____ TELEPHONE _____

H.A. "Humpy" Wheeler wasn't out to make history; he was looking to sell tickets. As president of the newly revamped Charlotte Motor Speedway, Wheeler was quickly becoming regarded as the P.T. Barnum of race promoters. In 1976, when Janet Guthrie failed to become the first woman qualifier for the Indy 500, her time trial was barely over when Wheeler had a plane in the air and a race car waiting in Charlotte, with a shot for her to race in his 1978 World 600.

Now an African-American racer named Willy T. Ribbs had caught Humpy's eye, and the wizard once again pulled a ride out of his hat, persuading engine builder Will Cronkrite to field a car for the sports car ace. Wheeler and Cronkrite took their Ford to the track for a practice session with Ribbs and waited for their driver … and waited … and waited.

Meanwhile, down in Charlotte, 20 minutes south, Ribbs had been arrested and bailed out for driving the wrong way on a one-way street. What was he doing downtown when he was supposed to be at the track, Cronkrite demanded? The angry owner was ready to walk away, but Wheeler would deliver.

There was this kid, a local racer, the son of short track legend Ralph Earnhardt. He was rough around the edges, but he could drive. At the very least, Wheeler thought, he'll show up.

Sure enough, Dale Earnhardt did show up.

And the rest is NASCAR history.

MAY 27 1978

THE PINCH-HITTER

THREE FOR THREE

OCTOBER 22, 1978

Tougher than a locust post, Cale Yarborough stood all of five-foot nothing and looked like he was built from tractor iron. During his fun-filled life, he had already survived a gunshot, a snake bite, a lightning strike, a parachute that had failed to open, and a wrestling match with an alligator.

Manhandling a two-ton race car? Child's play.

When Yarborough signed on with Junior Johnson, the owner's strategy was simple: "If we could build stuff that could keep up with Cale, there wasn't a race we couldn't win."

They won 13 races in 1974-75 but failed to finish 21 others, what with all the equipment falling apart under Cale's heavy foot. Then came 1976 and the start of perhaps the finest three-year stretch by a racing team in NASCAR's Modern Era: 90 races, 28 wins, 70 top-fives, and more than 10,000 laps led.

In the Sandhills of Rockingham, North Carolina, the No. 11 Oldsmobile capped off the Cale-Junior Era with one of the most devastating romps of the duo's career together, leading the final 352 laps of the 492-lap American 500. The win clinched the team's record-setting third straight Cup championship with two races left in the season.

It was a rout so devastating that nearly all of the 46,000 fans in attendance were long gone before the finish.

FEBRUAR

"AND THERE'S A FIGHT!"

As the green flag fell on the rain-delayed 21st running of the Daytona 500, it did so in front of 16 million viewers, who had tuned in for the first live flag-to-flag coverage of the Great American Race. They leaned forward as Donnie Allison took the white flag, with Cale Yarborough tucked in behind. They sat up in their La-Z-Boys as Donnie blocked Cale's slingshot move, hip-checking his rival into the infield grass. And they dropped their beers when Yarborough hung a hard right and slammed Allison into the Turn 3 wall.

Third-place A.J. Foyt, seeing the ruckus ahead, hesitated just long enough to allow Richard Petty and Darrell Waltrip to slip by. As Petty rocketed across the line for his sixth Daytona 500 victory, CBS announcer Ken Squier looked back to Turn 3.

"And there's a fight!" Squier shouted, as cameras captured the action. "It's Allison and Yarborough!"

An Allison was throwing punches, but it wasn't Donnie. Big brother Bobby says he strolled over, "and that's when Cale commenced to beating on my fist with his face."

The following day, NASCAR issued a statement saying that it "would not tolerate such behavior." But hidden behind that memo was an office full of smiles, a reaction topped only in the CBS production truck.

Ladies and gentlemen, this is NASCAR.

APRIL 1, 1979

RALPH'S BOY MAKES GOOD

All Dale Earnhardt wanted was a chance. Ever since his daddy had died, in 1973, Dale had wandered the racing earth looking for a steady ride.

But it didn't matter that Ralph Earnhardt had been a short track legend and a former NASCAR Sportsman Division champion.

It didn't even matter that Dale had run well when he replaced Willy T. Ribbs for four races.

What mattered was that no one was willing to put a race car in the hands of a dead-broke high school dropout with a reputation for orneriness. The third shift at the Fieldcrest-Cannon Plant 1 was calling Dale Earnhardt's name.

Enter one Rod Osterlund, a California-based real estate developer who decided it would be fun to own a Winston Cup team. When Humpy Wheeler offered him $5,000 to put a local racer in his car, he took the money and let Dale run a race in 1978. The following winter, Dale was in the No. 2 Chevy full-time.

In the seventh race of the 1979 season, the Southeastern 500 at Bristol, Earnhardt beat Bobby Allison by 2.7 seconds, becoming the first rookie to win in NASCAR's top series in five years.

"This is only a start," crew chief Jake "Suitcase" Elder told reporters. "If he don't get hurt, he's got at least 12 good years ahead of him."

Try 22.

DARLINGTON
APRIL 8, 1979

APRIL

WELCOME TO

Every decade or so, it seems, a pack of youngsters barges its way into the garage, raring to take over the joint. By 1979, the latest uprising had reached full song with the recent arrival of kids named Earnhardt, Labonte, Elliott, and Rudd. This new crew was headed up a brash Kentucky short-tracker named Darrell Waltrip.

From the first, DW's car was outrun only by his mouth, earning him a nickname from Cale Yarborough—Jaws—and a character assessment from Junior Johnson as "the perfect a—hole."

Jaws wasn't all mouth (or perfect, for that matter). But his sights were hard focused on the NASCAR throne, and he knew the only way to take it was to overthrow The King.

At the 1979 Rebel 500 in Darlington,

THE NEW BREED

Waltrip and Richard Petty traded the lead four times over the final lap, at the end of which DW made a gutsy crossover move to nail down the win. It was the beginning of a battle that would last until the season's final lap.

Lost in the frantic finish was a much more shocking conclusion. A miscommunication during a pit stop left David Pearson sitting behind the wheel of his Wood Brothers Mercury on pit road with no tires. It signaled a painful end to a long and successful rela-

tionship. A week later, Pearson was on the street, replaced by 33-year-old Neil Bonnett. Together, Pearson and Glen and Leonard Wood had won 43 races and 51 poles. Now apart, they began separate slides toward mediocrity and memories.

Darrell Waltrip, emboldened by his daring Darlington victory, won five of the 10 races between Memorial Day and Labor Day. Then, holding a massive championship lead over Petty, DW turned to a tactic he loved dearly: He started talking smack. DW questioned Petty's manhood. He joked about his age. He reminded everyone that the year before, for the first time since 1960, the No. 43 car hadn't won a single race.

Jaws was on a roll.

The King responded with uncharacteristic silence—and a very heavy foot.

With seven races remaining in the 1979 season, Waltrip's lead was 187 points. But when the teams gathered at the massive Ontario Motor Speedway in California for the season-ending L.A. Times 500, that margin was down to just two. Two hundred laps later, Petty topped Waltrip by three positions on the track and clinched his record-extending seventh Winston Cup title by a scant 11 points.

Afterward, the media fished for a parting shot from the aging King, a juicy quote to wrap the season and to teach that mouthy kid where the rubber meets the road.

It didn't happen.

What they didn't know was that Petty was eaten up with bleeding ulcers. Winning wasn't so easy anymore. This seventh title, capping the incredible comeback, had taken a heavy toll. A new decade, which would be his fifth in racing, was just around the corner.

Deep down, The King knew that Waltrip and the New Breed were right:

The times, they were a-changin'.

RACE SOFTLY, CARRY A BIG KICK

NOVEMBER

18

1979

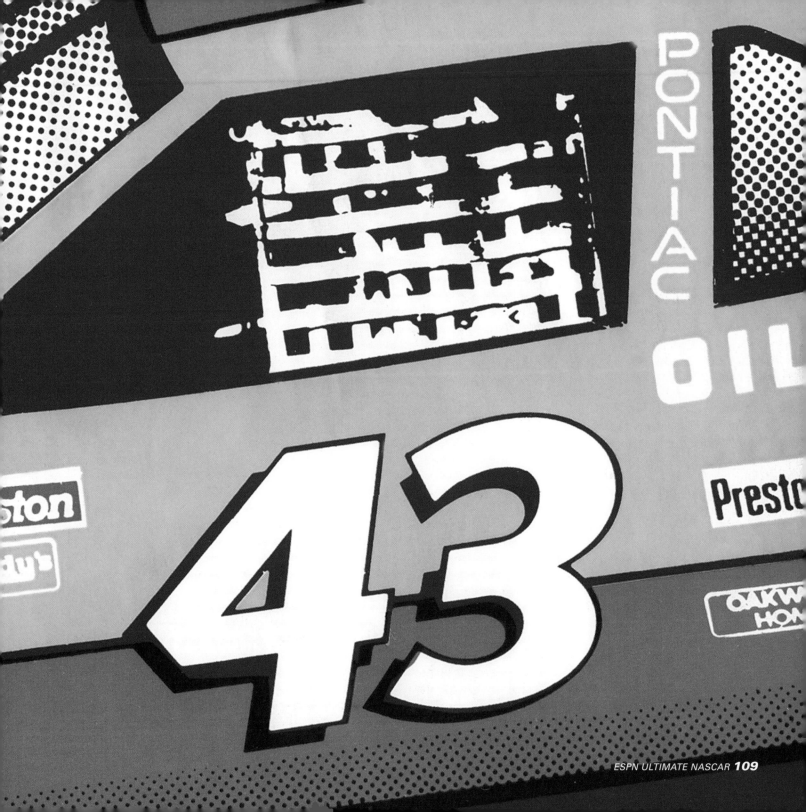

'80s

As the 20th century roared down the backstretch, NASCAR's version of the Greatest Generation began to act its age.

In the 1970s, David Pearson and Richard Petty combined to win 136 races. In the 1980s they would win 11, none after 1984. As the new decade began, Cale Yarborough secretly contemplated a semiretirement plan, too in love with his daughters to stay on the road 32 weeks a year.

Meanwhile, the sport's next generation was anxious to take the wheel from the old men's hands. In 1979, Dale Earnhardt won Rookie of the Year, Bill Elliott finished second to Pearson at Darlington, and Kyle Petty, son of Richard and grandson of Lee, started his first five races.

By the end of 1980, Rusty Wallace and Tim Richmond would also make their debuts. By the close of the decade, each would become a crucial part of NASCAR's move into the major leagues.

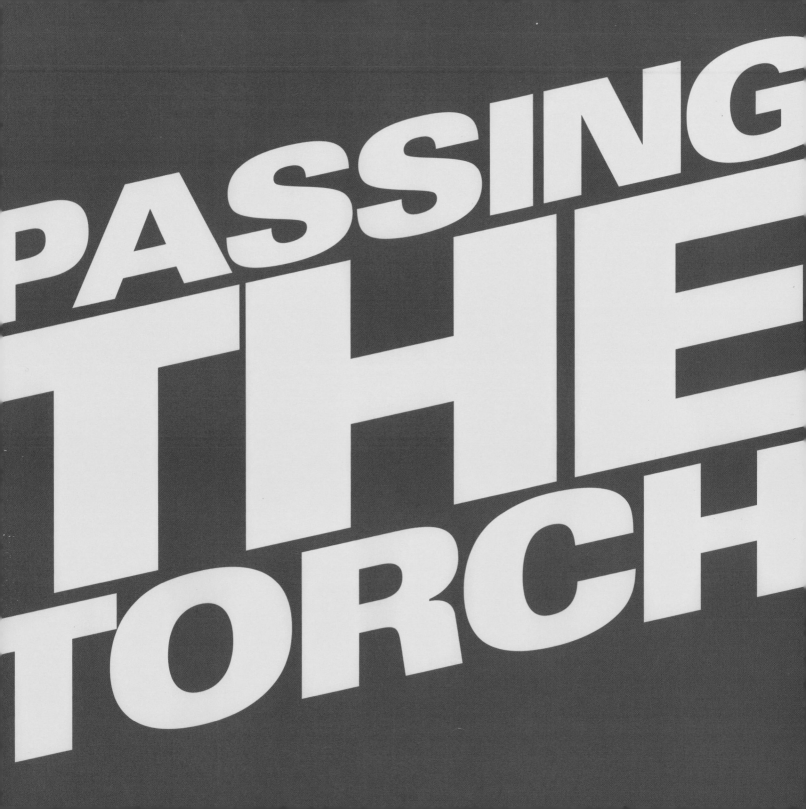

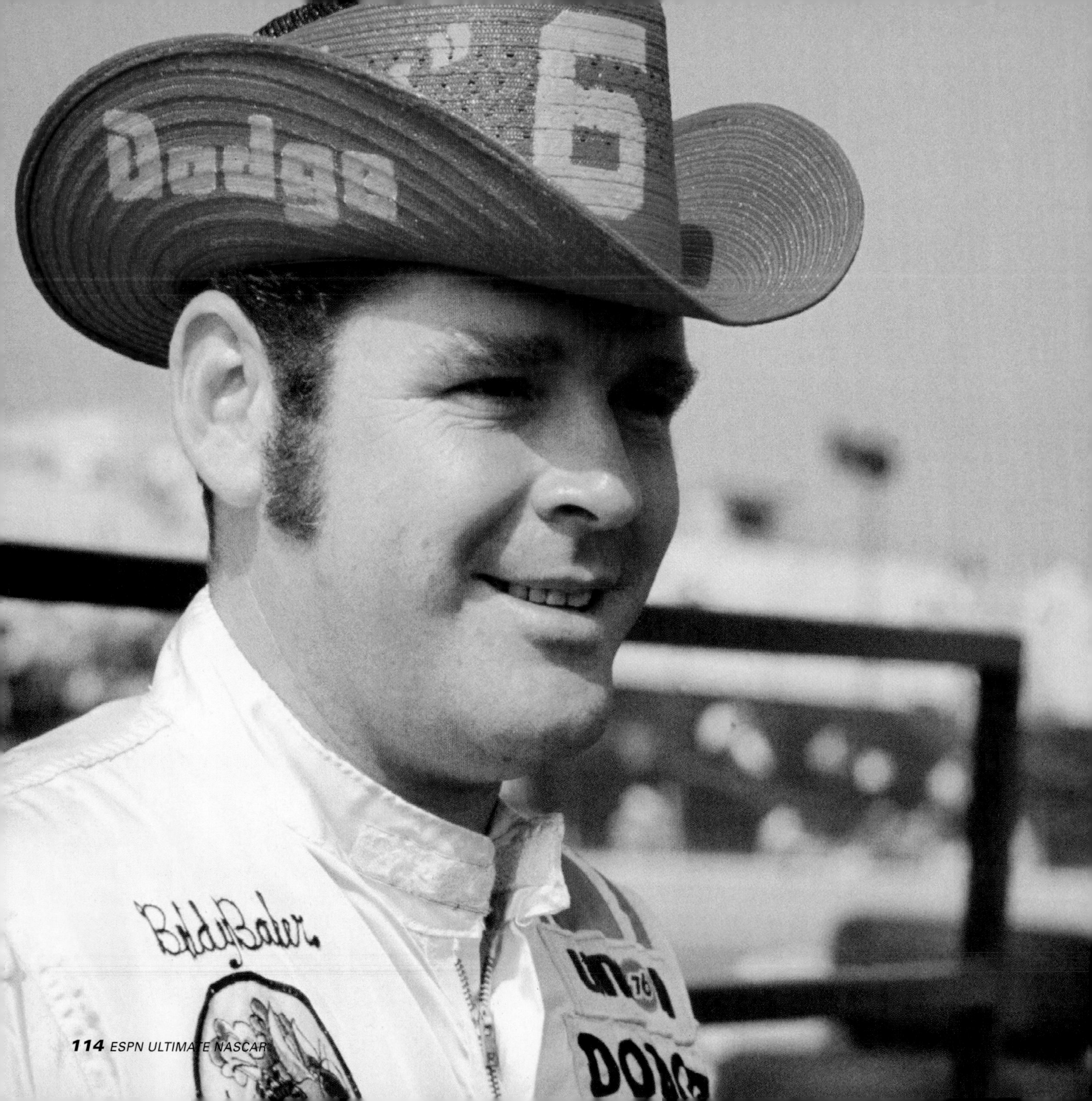
Dodge
6
Bobby Baker
76
DODG

FEBRUARY 17, 1980

"You really have to do something about Buddy Baker's car," the drivers begged NASCAR officials. "It's scaring the hell out of everybody."

Baker's ride was wicked fast, to be sure, but it was the car's color scheme that had everyone spooked. The Olds was painted a hue so similar to the Daytona asphalt that it disappeared like a chameleon, material-izing out of thin air. Dubbed the Gray Ghost, it proved to be the supernatural force that finally exorcised Baker's Daytona demons.

In 17 previous starts, Baker won the Daytona 480 more times than he cared to remember. It was the pesky Daytona 500 he had trouble with. Over seven tries between 1973 and 1979, he led six races and more than 330 laps but failed to finish five times.

Finally, in 1980, the Gray Ghost outran Baker's past, his bad luck, and 41 other cars. Baker led 143 of 200 laps and captured the flag with an average speed of 177.602 mph, the fastest Daytona 500 in history.

"I held down the throttle and held my breath," Baker said. "I figured the faster I got it over with, maybe I could get done before my luck got me again."

BEATING THE ODDS

When Rod Osterlund decided to take the plunge into Winston Cup racing, he knew he didn't have the cash and resources of the Wood Brothers, Petty Enterprises, or Junior Johnson. But what the Californian lacked in funding, he figured he'd make up for with pure, raw hunger. Not surprisingly, he built a team around that same quality.

Dale Earnhardt had already driven himself to near homelessness trying to become a racer, finally reaching a level of desperation sure to result in a little extra pressure on the accelerator on Sunday afternoon. Crew chief Doug Richert was barely 20 years old, too busy and too young to notice he was bringing a butter knife to a sword fight.

And yet, at the season-ending LA Times 500 in Ontario, Dale and Doug were competing against Cale Yarborough and Junior Johnson for the title. Two pitiful visits to Pit Road nearly cost the kids the Cup, but a nail-eating rally to a fifth-place finish clinched the championship by only 19 points. Earnhardt had become the first, and so far only, driver to back up a Rookie of the Year title with the Winston Cup.

"For the first time in my entire life I felt respected," Earnhardt said years later. "It was like I'd finally earned my place. But I knew I'd have to keep fighting to hang on to it."

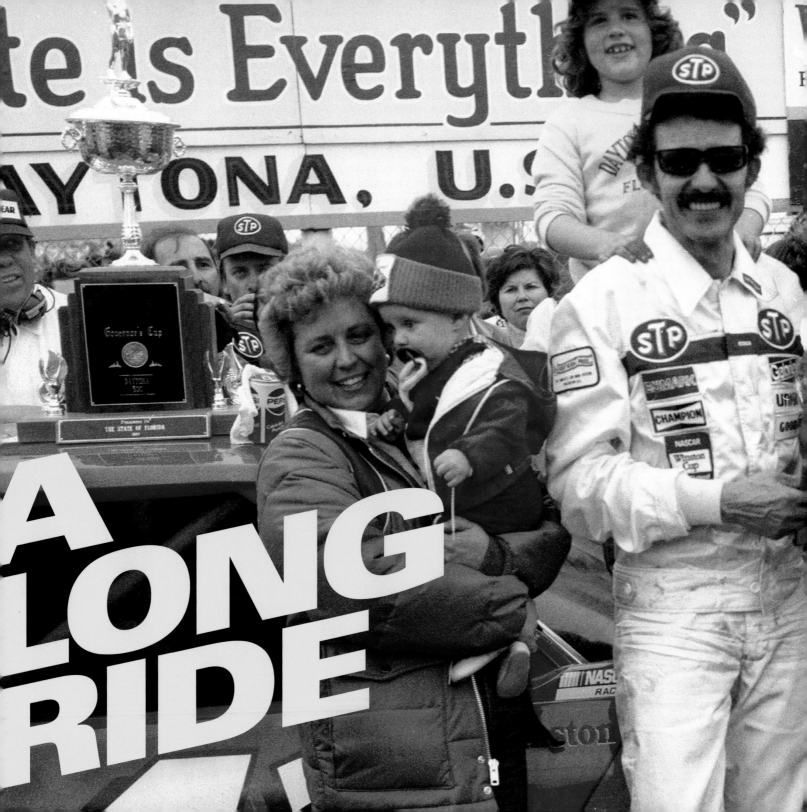

A LONG RIDE

As long as Richard Petty could remember, Dale Inman had been by his side, working to make Petty go faster, faster, faster. As kids, the cousins greased the axles of their red wagons to gain an edge on races down the hills of Randleman, North Carolina. When they got new bikes for Christmas, Dale stripped off the fenders and baskets to get them into "racing trim." So when they moved up to race cars, Richard slid behind the wheel while Dale crawled under the car.

Inman developed a rep as a magician of late-race strategy. Invariably, he pegged the perfect moments in a race for pit stops and, just as important, the times to push on a few extra few laps to steal an edge over the other racers. Inman's crew was the best of the best, always humming like a ... well-oiled machine.

After 192 wins, Richard never questioned Dale's judgment. So, with 25 laps left in the Daytona 500, the driver never hesitated when the crew chief relayed his plan.

"We were running fifth, and it was time to pit," Petty recalls. "Everyone else took gas and tires; Dale called for fuel only. We were in the pits less than eight seconds, and—bam!—we were gone. They never caught us."

The King won his seventh Daytona 500 thanks to one last great bit of advice from his cousin.

Two days later, Dale told Richard he was leaving the team. Inman, 44, needed to see if he could win away from the Petty empire.

"It didn't have anything to do with bad luck or bad feelings," Richard explained. "Dale just felt it was time for a change."

Maybe so, but without his cousin in his garage, Petty was once again headed downhill in a hurry.

"In 1980, we were the champions," Dale Earnhardt liked to say. "In 1981, we went to nothing."

As quickly as he had entered Winston Cup racing, Rod Osterlund was out. He'd wanted to prove to himself that he could come east and compete with the best. After two years, seven wins, and a championship, he'd made his point. Now he was gone.

No sooner than the team was sold to J.D. Stacy, Earnhardt followed his erstwhile partner out the door. "We" turned into "zero."

Along came Richard Childress, who understood Earnhardt's world. Childress had also clawed his way up through the sport, rising from the streets of Winston-Salem to become one of those bravest of NASCAR souls, an independent driver-owner. He bought, built, towed, and pitted his own race car, struggling all the while to make ends meet while competing against the Motown-backed superstars. In 12 years of Cup racing, Childress had six top-five finishes and no wins. But damn it, he was living the dream.

At a powwow in Anniston, Alabama, on the outskirts of Talladega, Dale and RC discussed their situations. Childress had the car; Earnhardt had the driving talent. Maybe they should give it a try, no commitments, to see if they could stand working together. So the two agreed to work together for the remainder of the 1981 season.

The rest, as they say, is NASCAR history.

"Richard got out of his own car and allowed the champion to save face," Earnhardt recalled more than a decade later. "If he hadn't stepped in, I might have disappeared forever. From that point on, I was indebted to him for the rest of my life."

It was a debt that Dale would pay in full, as he and RC went on to build the greatest dynasty NASCAR has ever seen.

AUGUST 1, 1981

1+1

28-CALE YARBOROUGH
RACECAM

RIDING SHOTGUN

The trip to Australia was a disaster. Ken Squier had traveled to Sydney to broadcast the 1980 Mr. Olympia contest for CBS Sports, only to have his color commentator, Arnold Schwarzenegger, bail on the telecast and enter the event as a competitor.

"Arnold wasn't in great shape since he'd retired to make movies," Squier later recalled, "so when he won, it made the other guys mad. The second-place finisher smashed his trophy onto the floor. It was a mess."

To wipe the experience from their minds, Squier and the crew drove west to the racing hotbed of Bathurst. That's when Squier saw it: a TV camera, built for sailboat racing, mounted inside the race cars. "I called CBS and said, 'We have to have this.' "

The monster was seated alongside Cale Yarborough during the 1983 Daytona 500, bolted to the roll cage inside his No. 28 Pontiac LeMans. For three hours it swiveled left and right, looking out all four windows at 200 mph. When Cale whipped around Buddy Baker with one lap to go, the television audience rode with him, watching Baker's Ford fall helplessly backward.

As he crossed the finish line for his third 500 victory, Yarborough waved to the camera and shouted, "Thank you, CBS!"

Up in the broadcast booth, Squier very likely thought to himself, Thank you, Mr. Schwarzenegger.

Bobby Allison hated Darrell Waltrip. Didn't dislike him. Didn't merely not care for him. He hated him.

The animosity first heated up on the Deep South short tracks of Alabama and Tennessee. It smoldered when Waltrip became a Cup contender in the late 1970s. By 1983, it had boiled over into seething disgust. The previous two seasons Bobby had squandered big points leads down the stretch, and both times DW had been the beneficiary.

Now it was happening again. With five races to go, Allison's lead was over 100 points. Entering the season finale, the Winston Western 500 in Riverside, California, the margin had shrunk to 64, a mere nine positions on the racetrack.

A flat tire came first, followed by a mysterious drop in fuel pressure and a strange engine knock. With 11 laps to go, Bobby was stuck in 20th while Waltrip ran up front. But a Tim Richmond-aided spin sent Darrell into the dirt and allowed Allison to close the gap. When the race was over, Bobby had outlasted DW by 47 points for his lone Winston Cup title.

Over two decades later, Allison still can't resist taking a shot at his old rival: "We discovered that someone had poured a 10-pound sack of sugar into the gas tank, stopping up everything like it was sand. I'm not saying who probably did it. Then again, I probably don't have to, do I?"

PART-TIME

ROMP

For 38 laps, Darrell Waltrip drove with one eye straight ahead and the other in his rear-view mirror. The view never changed in either direction. Up ahead was nothing but empty track, a peaceful view for a man still searching for his first Daytona 500 win. It was the scenery behind his No. 11 Chevy that had DW worried.

Filling the mirror was the bright orange hood of Cale Yarborough's No. 28 car, bouncing up and down over the bumps of the 2.5-mile superspeedway. That meant trouble for DW.

Cale was a part-time racer now, spending most of his time at home in Timmonsville, South Carolina, looking after his daughters and his investments. He went racing only when the checks were fat and the trophies tall. In 1983, he hit the track only 16 times, but he won on four occasions.

Junior Johnson had questioned Cale's decision to quit his team in 1980, which had emptied the cockpit that Waltrip now occupied. Plenty of others agreed that Yarborough's retreat was a mistake.

In yet another signature slingshot move, Yarborough shut them all up. The 43-year-old stay-at-home dad snaked around DW to engrave his name on the Harley J. Earl Trophy for the fourth time, second only to Richard Petty's seven.

Then Cale went back to Timmonsville to be with his girls. Later, he'd come back to race again—and he'd whip 'em all again. But now it was time to go home.

APRIL 1, 1984

THUNDER AND LIGHTNING When the Bristol Motor Speedway was built in 1960, the half-mile track was literally carved into the East Tennessee hills, creating a dark, steep bowl. Its turns eventually became banked in a nearly straight uphill 36°, the steepest in NASCAR.

Once 30 race cars were unleashed onto the track's surface, superlatives rolled out faster than a 15-second lap. One driver claimed it was "like flying fighter jets in a high school gymnasium," while another likened it to "racing semis in a cereal bowl." All agreed on the perfect nickname: Thunder Valley, USA.

This was Junior Johnson's kind of place. He'd learned how to race while hauling illegal liquids through these very hills, and he'd won at Thunder Valley as a driver in 1965. But the way Johnson stamped his name on the joint—literally—was as a car owner.

From 1971 to 1984, Johnson-owned cars won 19 of 26 races run in Thunder Valley. Darrell Waltrip's win in the 1984 Valleydale 500 was the eighth consecutive Thunder Valley triumph for a Johnson-owned car, a streak that started in 1980 with Cale Yarborough behind the wheel. Now Waltrip won his seventh in a row at Thunder Valley, tying him with Richard Petty (Richmond, 1970-73) for the longest one-track streak for any driver in NASCAR history.

No wonder a modern-day visit to the Bristol Motor Speedway begins with a view of the aptly named Junior Johnson Grandstand.

Lap	#	Leader		Lap	#	Leader		Lap	#	Leader
1	#9	Bill Elliott		2	#28	Cale Yarborough		3	#28	Cale Yarborough
4	#28	Cale Yarborough		5	#3	Dale Earnhardt		6	#55	Benny Parsons
7	#55	Benny Parsons		8	#55	Benny Parsons		9	#55	Benny Parsons
10	#21	Buddy Baker		11	#21	Buddy Bal…		23	#55	Benny Parsons
24	#21	Buddy Baker		25	#55	Benny Parsons		26	#55	Benny Parsons
27	#55	Benny Parsons		28	#21	Buddy Baker		29	#55	Benny Parsons
30	#55	Benny Parsons		31	#55	Benny Parsons		32	#22	Bobby Allison
33	#28	Cale Yarbor…		39	#22	Bobby Allison		40	#22	Bobby Allison
41	#43	Richard Petty		42	#43	Richard Petty		43	#43	Richard Petty
44	#22	Bobby Allison		45	#22	Bobby Allison		46	#21	Buddy Baker
47	#21	Buddy Baker		48	#21	Buddy Baker		49	#28	Cale Yarbor…
55	#22	Bobby Allison		56	#22	Bobby Allison		57	#43	Richard Petty
58	#21	Buddy Baker		59	#21	Buddy Baker		60	#21	Buddy Baker
61	#43	Richard Petty		62	#21	Buddy Baker		63	#88	Rusty Wallace
64	#66	Phil Parsons		65	#66	Phil Pars…		71	#55	Benny Parsons
72	#55	Benny Parsons		73	#55	Benny Parsons		74	#55	Benny Parsons
75	#55	Benny Parsons		76	#55	Benny Parsons		77	#55	Benny Parsons
78	#44	Terry Labonte		79	#44	Terry Labonte		80	#43	Richard Petty
81	#43	Richard P…		87	#16	David Pearson		88	#16	David Pearson
89	#43	Richard Petty		90	#43	Richard Petty		91	#43	Richard Petty
92	#43	Richard Petty		93	#43	Richard Petty		94	#22	Bobby Allison
95	#21	Buddy Baker		96	#21	Buddy Baker		97	#55	Benny Par…
103	#55	Benny Parsons		104	#55	Benny Parsons		105	#55	Benny Parsons
106	#55	Benny Parsons		107	#47	Ron Bouchard		108	#21	Buddy Baker
109	#47	Ron Bouchard		110	#47	Ron Bouchard		111	#55	Benny Parsons
112	#55	Benny Parsons		113	#55	Benny Pa…		119	#44	Terry Labonte
120	#55	Benny Parsons		121	#55	Benny Parsons		122	#55	Benny Parsons
123	#21	Buddy Baker		124	#21	Buddy Baker		125	#21	Buddy Baker
126	#55	Benny Parsons		127	#55	Benny Parsons		128	#21	Buddy Baker
129	#21	Buddy B…		135	#21	Buddy Baker		136	#21	Buddy Baker
137	#21	Buddy Baker		138	#55	Benny Parsons		139	#21	Buddy Baker
140	#21	Buddy Baker		141	#55	Benny Parsons		142	#55	Benny Parsons
143	#21	Buddy Baker		144	#21	Buddy Baker		145	#21	Buddy B…
151	#28	Cale Yarborough		152	#28	Cale Yarborough		153	#44	Terry Labonte
154	#44	Terry Labonte		155	#44	Terry Labonte		156	#44	Terry Labonte
157	#55	Benny Parsons		158	#55	Benny Parsons		159	#55	Benny Parsons
160	#55	Benny Parsons		161	#55	Benny Pa…		167	#21	Buddy Baker
168	#55	Benny Parsons		169	#55	Benny Parsons		170	#21	Buddy Baker
171	#55	Benny Parsons		172	#55	Benny Parsons		173	#33	Harry Gant
174	#21	Buddy Baker		175	#33	Harry Gant		176	#33	Harry Gant
177	#33	Harry G…								

CURSE? WHAT CURSE?

On Nov. 9, 1813, Andrew Jackson led 2,000 troops into eastern Alabama to rid the area of its original inhabitants, the Creek Indians. Legend says that a medicine man placed a curse on the land as he was marched away. That land is now inhabited by the Talladega Superspeedway.

Tales of the curse have long dogged the track, from the boycott of 1969 to the death of Tiny Lund, in 1975. In the middle of a 1973 race, NASCAR champion Bobby Isaac pulled off the track while leading, climbed from his car, and walked off, claiming that a voice had told him to do so.

As the track entered its 16th season, its very existence was in question. Was it too fast? Too big? Too dangerous? Was the curse more than mere legend?

Then came three glorious hours of racing in the 1984 Winston 500. Thirteen drivers swapped the lead a mind-bending 75 times, and that was only the official count at the start-finish line. The actual count throughout every corner of the 2.66-mile behemoth? Close to 150.

The day's leader list included names like Petty, Allison, Earnhardt, Baker, Labonte, Parsons (Benny and little brother Phil), Wallace, and Elliott. In the end, Cale Yarborough overtook Harry Gant on the final lap.

"People paid good money for those seats," Cale said afterward. "But I don't think they ever actually used them."

MAY 6, 1984

JULY 4, 1984   HAIL TO THE KING >>>

>>> After a lifetime of winning, Richard Petty saw a two-decade race to 200 career wins grinding down to an excruciating crawl.

Starting the 1982 season with 195 wins, Petty had nine top-five finishes but no checkered flags. He won three times in 1983, but the third win came despite two rules violations, an oversized engine and two illegal tires. NASCAR let the victory stand, but handed Petty a scarlet letter by stripping him of both points and cash. For the first time in his career, The King wrestled with public disgrace.

The following year, win 199 finally came, at Dover. That set the stage for the biggest Fourth of July celebration in NASCAR history.

At the Firecracker 400 at Daytona Beach, President Ronald Reagan made history by becoming the first sitting president to attend a NASCAR event. Not that he did much sitting, what with Petty and old foe Cale Yarborough banging doors as they barreled off Turn 4 and screamed over the finish line. ABC Sports cameras revealed that the No. 43 had won by inches. The wait for 200 had finally ended.

No one knew at the time that it would be Petty's final trip to Victory Lane. Even if they had, they wouldn't have cared. There was a celebration to be thrown and a picnic in the garage, complete with a King and a President going elbow to elbow in a family size bucket of Kentucky Fried Chicken.

"I won my race," Petty, a longtime Republican, told the man standing next to him, who was up for reelection that fall. "Now you go win yours."

See, here's the thing about trying to stop a train—you can hear it coming for miles, see it coming for minutes, and pile anything you want on the tracks in front of it, but you know exactly what the train knows: There's nothing you can do to stop it.

TRULY AWESOME

205.114 mph

EBRUARY 17, 1985

When Bill Elliott unloaded his No. 9 Coors Ford for preseason testing at Daytona on Jan. 2, a chill rippled through the garage. The damn thing looked fast just sitting there, like a bright red bullet. The first time No. 9 hit the track, it topped 202 mph. Everyone else was struggling to hit 200.

Just one month later, during qualifying for the Daytona 500, Elliott's T-Bird won the pole at 205.114, nearly 2 mph faster than second-place qualifier Cale Yarborough. When the Great American Race began, Cale kept up for 62 laps, until his engine blew apart under the stress of matching pace with Elliott. By the race's end, 21 others would follow Yarborough behind the wall, their cars and spirits broken.

A stunned Elliott stood in Victory Lane certain that this would be the greatest achievement of his racing career. Truth is, Awesome Bill was just getting going.

MILLION DOLLAR BILL

Awesome Bill Elliott steamrolled his way through the 1985 season, winning 10 of the first 20 events, including a startling two-lap comeback at Talladega in May.

With two of four "crown jewel" events in the bag, he arrived in Darlington for the Southern 500 with a chance to win the Winston Million—as in $1 million, a nice little bonus that rounded out the largest one-day paycheck in racing history.

The sport had never received so much attention—and neither had the reluctant, reclusive Elliott. ESPN cameras dogged his every step. Photographers and reporters and guys with mikes encircled him. *Sports Illustrated* prepared to go with its first NASCAR cover since 1977. At one point, when the media trapped him at his car, Elliott dropped to his knees and slid underneath it. Darlington officials eventually brought in a police escort to keep the crowds at bay. And all that was before the race.

For 500 miles, Awesome Bill dodged an obstacle course littered with trouble. His car handled terribly, he missed a spinning Dale Earnhardt by inches, and he narrowly avoided a wreck with Cale Yarborough with only 43 laps to go.

Finally, when he sailed past the checkered flag, the roar of the crowd was outdone only by the sigh of relief from the cockpit. "I'm just glad it's over," said the man from Dawsonville, Georgia, standing in a rain of dollar bills and looking like a deer caught in headlights. Then, suddenly brightening, he smiled: "But I'll take the money."

$1,000,000

FEBRUARY 23, 1986

It took five years, but the Earnhardt-Childress team was finally fulfilling its promise. After a handful of wins, a dumpster of blown engines, even a little time apart, Dale and RC were ready to make a run at the title. To win it, though, they would have to go through Darrell Waltrip.

And so, on a bone-hardening winter day in Richmond, at the Miller High Life 400, Dale did just that.

For most of the race, Earnhardt's Wrangler Chevy kept Waltrip's Bud machine stuck in second place. In every turn, Darrell dived and Dale blocked, their left-side tires covered in cold infield mud.

With three laps to go, Waltrip spotted—no, forced—an opening, then snaked his way to the inside and into the lead. To no one's great surprise, Dale promptly nailed him. Both cars lost control and hit the Turn 3 wall with such force that the metal guardrail was shredded. The crash took out the first four cars, scattering smashed parts and hurt feelings all across the backstretch.

Only one lead-lap car managed to navigate through the debris field. It was driven by a 25-year-old kid who, though earning just his first win, was already plenty familiar with the Richmond winner's circle. His grandfather had won there twice. His father was the track's all-time win leader with 13.

Now Kyle Petty had made his family the sport's first three-generation winners.

FAMILY WAY

Ernie Elliott never envied his little brother. When the Elliott boys rolled out of Dawsonville, Georgia, to go NASCAR racing in 1976, Bill did the driving and Ernie provided the horsepower. Bill dealt (albeit reluctantly) with reporters, sponsors, and autograph hounds, while Ernie looked to squeeze one more horse out of his immaculately crafted engines. Bill got public credit for winning two Daytona 500s and 21 poles, but the first thing to cross the finish line each time was always an Ernie Elliott power plant. Ernie was perfectly happy with that division of labor.

E ENVELOPE
APRIL 30, 1987

So when it came time to qualify for the 1987 Winston 500 at Talladega, it wasn't a question of whether the Elliott clan would win the pole but by how much. But no one, not in the wildest racing dream, could have predicted the number that flashed onto the scoreboard: 212.809.

"You think these cars can go faster than that?" a reporter asked Ernie after the mind-boggling feat.

"Sure," the big brother replied. "I don't see anything keeping us from going faster."

Nothing did.

MAY 3, 1987

All Bobby Allison heard was a big bang. His No. 22 Miller High Life ride was hurtling alongside the longest grandstand in the world in the Winston 500 at Talladega at more than 200 mph when the engine self-destructed so violently that the entire crankshaft blew out of the bottom of the Buick, launching the car into the air.

Allison's 3,600-pound machine smashed into the frontstretch catch fence with such violence that the railing exploded, rocketing metal shards into the grandstand as the race car—or what was left of it—helicoptered back onto the track.

As the 49-year-old driver sat stunned on the asphalt, his face covered in oil, he asked safety crews how many fans had been killed. None, they said, but he didn't believe them. It had been too violent. In truth, only five fans had been hurt, and only two of them needed attention at area hospitals.

Even as he watched his son Davey take the victory hours later, Bobby knew that NASCAR would react swiftly and decisively. They did, introducing the restrictor plate, a piece of aluminum that choked engines and cut horsepower in half.

The drivers didn't like the idea, but the images of Talladega, the gaping hole in the fence, the terror on the faces of fans—and the unspeakable horror of what might have been—placed a restrictor plate on their complaining.

UNRESTRICTED HORROR

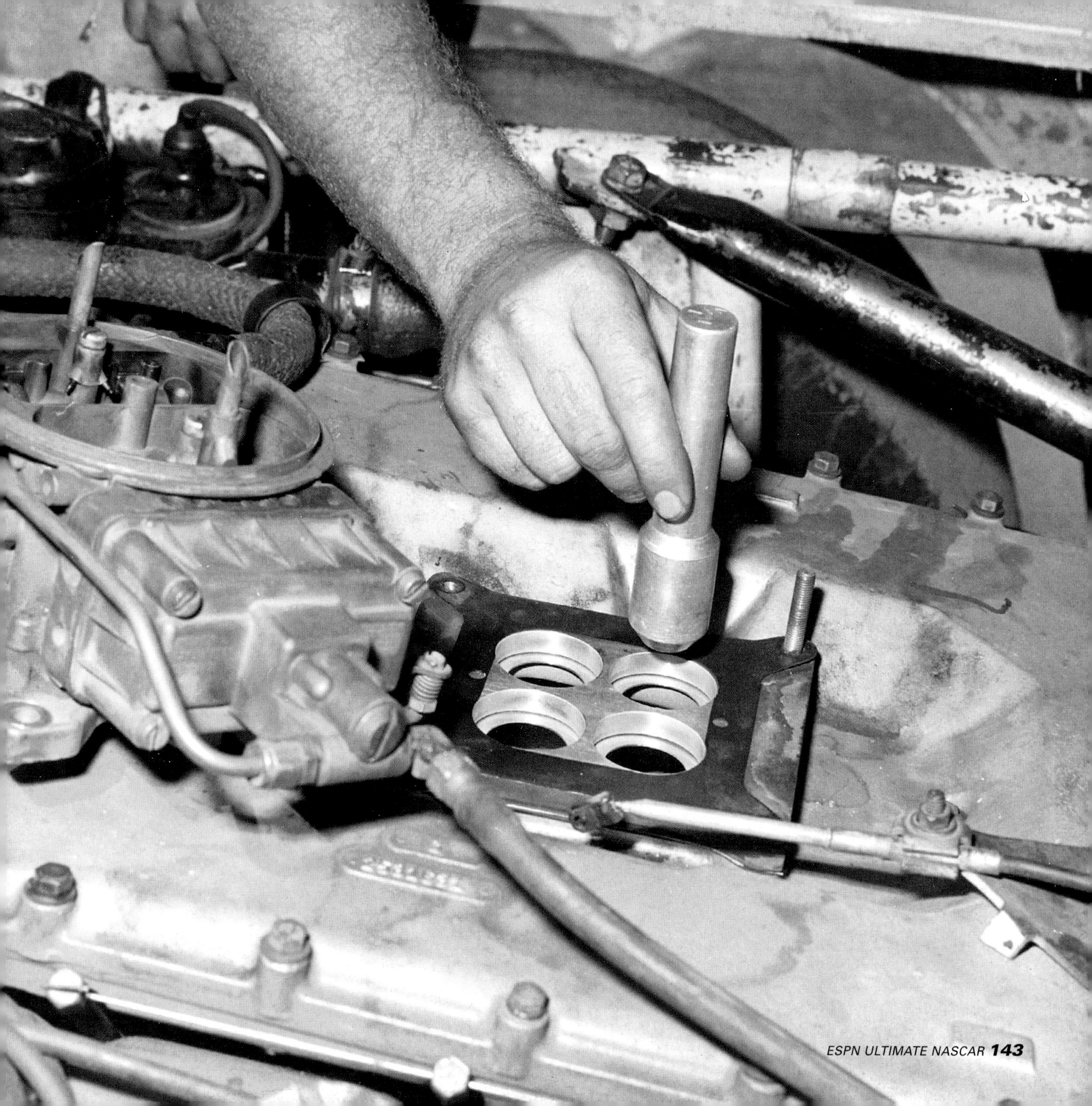

In 1985, R.J. Reynolds persuaded NASCAR to stage an all-star event featuring race winners from the previous season. NASCAR obliged, but for two years, the race put fans to sleep. In 1986, only 18,500 spectators showed up, prompting Darrell Waltrip to wonder aloud if it might be quicker to introduce the fans to the drivers during the prerace ceremonies instead of the other way around.

Maybe, RJR began to think, this wasn't such a great idea. But the company decided to give it another try in 1987.

This time, after races of 75 and 50 laps to determine position for the final 10-lap sprint for the $200,000 first-place prize, the scene at the Charlotte Motor Speedway turned into something straight out of 1949.

Bill Elliott and Geoff Bodine hit each other. Dale Earnhardt spun Bodine. Earnhardt blocked Elliott, so Elliott hit him. As the pair traveled down the frontstretch, they made contact again. This time, Earnhardt's Chevy went into the grass, normally a disastrous situation with a fast car, treadless tires, and damp sod.

But the No. 3 car simply slid sideways, righted itself, and blew back onto the track to retake the lead. Dale won, Bill fumed, and for reasons no one could explain, Richard Petty had to break up a fight in the garage between Rusty Wallace and Kyle Petty.

One writer called it "an ugly and shameful day for Winston Cup racing." But the grandstand had been galvanized, and a new hero had been born. The pilot of the No. 3 car had come to Charlotte as Dale Earnhardt. He left as The Intimidator.

MAY 17, 1987

PASS
IN THE
GRASS

JUNE 14, 1987
SHOOTING STAR

Tim Richmond never really fit in. A native of Ohio, the former Indy 500 Rookie of the Year strutted a balls-out driving style topped for daring only by his lifestyle. He traveled in a tricked-out RV with an expandable party suite, entertained an army of women, and dreamed of being an actor.

Oh, and one more thing—the son of a gun could flat out drive a race car.

In 1986, his first year with car owner Rick Hendrick, Richmond led the circuit with seven wins and finished third in points be-hind Dale Earnhardt and Darrell Waltrip. But at the start of the 1987 season, Richmond wasn't around. Over the winter, he'd con-tracted what he called "Asian flu." Rumors swirled that he'd partied himself into the ground, that he was hooked on cocaine.

The truth was worse.

Richmond returned for the Miller High Life 500 at the triangular Pocono Raceway, where he'd won three times before, twice the previous year. This time it was no con-test: Richmond led the final 47 laps to earn the eighth win in his last 18 starts. One week later he won again, on the road course at Riverside, spurring talk of the greatest comeback in NASCAR history.

What fans and friends could see down on Victory Lane was a miraculous celebra-tion by a jubilant victor. What they didn't see were the race-morning blood transfu-sions, the near-violent mood swings, and the agony of a man who needed help just getting out of bed in the morning.

Images of a dying man.

More than in any other sport, family connects the world of auto racing. It's a world where last names are more famous than firsts. As one branch falls from the family tree, another inevitably grows to take its place.

For the Allison family, that second generation arrived in 1987 in the form of David Carl Allison, the eldest son of Bobby and Judy. That year Davey, 26, posted the most successful rookie season in NASCAR history, earning two wins and five poles. The following year, in just his 31st career start, Davey had a chance to win the Daytona 500, running second with one lap to go. The leader was a two-time 500 winner with long, gray sideburns peaking out from beneath his helmet. His name? Bobby Allison.

Davey moved high and low, straining for a final run, but the old man was too fast and won by two car lengths. As they slowed for the cooldown lap, onboard cameras captured Bobby's 50-year-old hand reaching out through the window to wave at his boy.

Victory Lane was a family affair. Bobby talked about the thrill of seeing Davey make a charge. Davey declared the second-place finish "the greatest victory of my career." And when asked whom she'd pulled for, Judy—the runner-up's mom—declared, "Bobby. He's the one who pays the bills."

Just four months later, the party was over.

FAMILY OUTING

FEBRUARY
14
1988

JUNE 19, 1988

BOBBY SAYS GOOD-BYE Forty cars were rocketing through the second of Pocono Raceway's three turns in the Miller High Life 500 when the radio call came to the pit from Bobby Allison: "I think I've got a tire going down ... "

Seconds later, Allison's No. 12 Miller High Life car looped around backward and hit the metal wall at the entrance of Turn 2. The Buick came to rest in the middle of the track, directly in the path of journeyman Jocko Maggiacomo, who plowed into Allison's window at 180 mph.

As the field drove back by the wreck under caution, Davey Allison saw his father slumped backward, surrounded by the paramedics who had scrambled into the car to perform an emergency tracheotomy. Moments later, Bobby was airlifted to nearby Allentown with what was listed as "cerebral concussion, blunt abdominal trauma, and broken thighbone."

Fans and family held vigil outside Lehigh Valley Memorial, none expecting Bobby to see morning. But he survived the night, the week, and then the next month. He woke from his coma. Slowly, painfully slowly, he regained the ability to talk, eat, bathe, and walk. By the following February, the defending Daytona 500 champion walked into the garage to a chorus of cheers.

His driving career was over, and every step was now charged full of pain, every sentence a chore. But damned if Bobby Allison wasn't alive, driven by the dream to see his sons become racing champions.

A dream that would become an unfathomable nightmare.

'I WON THE DAYTONA 500!'

Darrell Waltrip was feeling beaten down. He was 42 years old, and his three championship trophies were collecting dust. So owner Rick Hendrick brought in Waltrip's crew chief from his glory days with Junior Johnson, Jeff "Hollywood" Hammond. Good move. And just in time for the Great American Race.

The field was all spread out, and with 35 laps to go and 18 laps since their last pit stop, DW and Hollywood figured the race might stay green the rest of the way. "Hollywood told me if I was light on the throttle, we could make it on fuel," Waltrip recalls. "So I started a-dancin' on that pedal."

One by one, the leaders pitted for gas. Finally, with four laps to go, Waltrip's No. 17 Chevy took the lead for the first time all day. Drafting off anyone and anything he could find, DW squeezed 132.5 miles out of one tank of fuel, snapping an 0-for-17 Daytona jinx and running out of gas as he rolled into Victory Lane. "I won the Daytona 500! I won the Daytona 500!" NASCAR's fastest mouth babbled. "This is the Daytona 500, isn't it? Don't tell me it isn't! Thank God!"

MEET RUSTY WALLACE

If ever there was a candidate to take the fast-mouth mantle from Darrell Waltrip, it was Russell Wallace of St. Louis. Rusty made his first Cup start in 1980, finishing second to Dale Earnhardt at Atlanta, and in 1988, he missed winning the championship by only 24 points to Bill Elliott.

He was young, mad, and didn't much care what anyone thought about him. He reminded Waltrip of, well, himself. Now, with a little more than two miles remaining in the Winston, Rusty did Darrell a great favor: He jerked the black hat right off DW's head.

Running 1-2 as they approached the white flag, Wallace crept up to Waltrip's rear deck in the middle of Turns 3 and 4. Then, in plain view of a grandstand of eyewitnesses, Wallace spun Waltrip out. As the 32-year-old Wallace won the race, the checkered flag was joined by a shower of beer cans, chicken bones, and various other projectiles that angry fans could get their hands on. In the garage, Waltrip's crew lined up shoulder to shoulder, blocking the entrance to Victory Lane. Shouts turned to shoves, shoves led to punches, and a 20-man melee broke out.

"Next morning, my kids came upstairs," Wallace remembers. "They said, 'Dad, how come there are cops in our driveway?' I said, 'Don't worry, there's just a few people mad at your dad this morning.'"

Actually, an entire nation was hopping mad. NASCAR Nation.

Their new favorite villain had arrived.

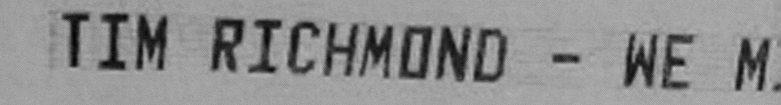
TIM RICHMOND - WE M

AUGUST 13, 1989
DEATH OF A BROTHER

The shouts that had pushed Tim Richmond around the Indianapolis Motor Speedway, the booming applause that had shaken Victory Lane visits from Darlington to Daytona, were no more. The only sounds Richmond heard now were the chattering of nurses in the hallway, the beep-beep of a heart monitor, and the Darth Vader-like wheezing of a respirator.

Now Richmond was in a West Palm Beach hospital bed, waiting to die.

No one from NASCAR had called or visited Richmond in more than a year, not since his mysterious disappearance from the garage. The amazing comeback of 1987 had started with two wins, then slowly degenerated into erratic behavior and sudden mood swings. NASCAR, suspecting a drug problem, had suspended Richmond in early 1988. He knew the accusations weren't true, but he was too sick to fight anymore.

S YOU — YOUR FANS

What no one knew at the time was that Richmond's erratic behavior and sudden mood swings weren't the result of recreational drugs, but rather the side effects of AZT and other treatments used to combat AIDS. Richmond had known about his condition since December 1986, a full seven months before his comeback victory at Pocono. But the racer was well aware of the stigma that comes with those four letters, and he kept the news under wraps.

Now, less than three years later, his 200 mph lifestyle came to claim its due. At 5:12 a.m. on a Sunday morning, Tim Richmond died quietly. He was 34.

Roughly 12 hours later, after winning the Winston Cup race at Watkins Glen, Rusty Wallace dedicated the win to Richmond. Wallace didn't know at the time that his old rival was dead. No one outside Richmond's immediate family knew until the following day.

It just seemed like the right thing to do.

15TH
NEVER
LOOKED
SO GOOD

NOVEMBER 19, 1989

If Rusty Wallace could stay within 19 positions of Dale Earnhardt in the season-capping Atlanta Journal 500, the Winston Cup title would finally be his.

"It sounded easy enough at the time," Wallace says now. "But I never worked so damn hard in my life."

His No. 27 Kodiak Pontiac was handling like a cranky washing machine, and Wallace quickly fell one lap behind Earnhardt. Then a tire went flat. Next a set of lug nuts chewed through a wheel rim. Wallace fell to 33rd before rallying to finish an ugly 15th.

Dale won the race, but Rusty—never so happy to be 14 cars behind a checkered flag—won the Cup. The margin: 12 points.

Just as the Cup validated Wallace's career, so the decade validated NASCAR's arrival as a major sport.

Ten years earlier, only one Winston Cup race had been broadcast in its entirety. In 1989, ABC, CBS, ESPN, and various cable channels carried all 29 events, from green flag to checkered. The result? A nation of new fans, including a generation of youngsters who grew up dreaming of becoming the next Rusty or Dale.

'90s

As the century entered its final decade, forces within and around the sport of stock car racing began a sort of harmonic convergence. NASCAR no longer had to plead with TV execs to get its races on air; networks now came to NASCAR with millions in cash in their trunks to pay for the privilege. Geographic walls came tumblin' down as investors began to build new racetracks on the outskirts of Los Angeles, Dallas, Miami, and Las Vegas. And in the summer of 1990, the hot movie was *Days of Thunder*, starring Tom Cruise and Robert Duvall, who turned down a *Godfather* sequel to play a crew chief.

What's more, the open-wheel empire in Indianapolis was on the brink of disaster, soon to collapse under its own political weight. Indy's arrogant ways had forced rising star Jeff Gordon southward into stock cars, a world hitherto dominated by blue-collar heroes driving mean, black machines—Rusty, Davey, and Dale.

Gordon's driving style, West Coast manner, and Hollywood looks drew curious stares from every corner of the garage. Soon, the kid who didn't fit in would become the face of his sport, bringing with him a new audience and saving NASCAR from a year of unbearable tragedy.

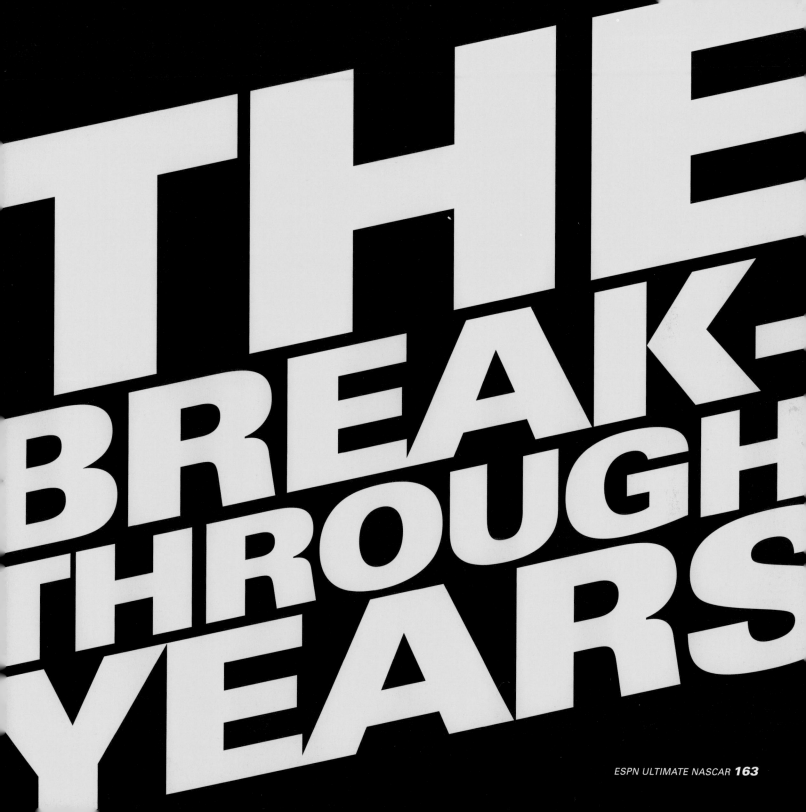

THE BREAK-THROUGH YEARS

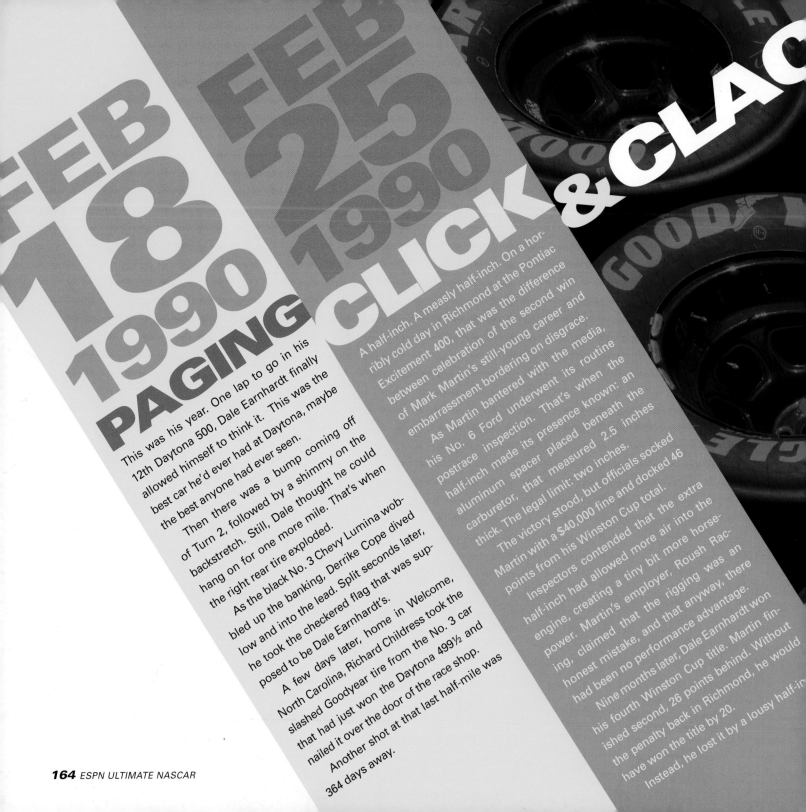

FEB 18 1990

PAGING CLICK & CLAC

This was his year. One lap to go in his 12th Daytona 500, Dale Earnhardt finally allowed himself to think it. This was the best car he'd ever had at Daytona, maybe the best anyone had ever seen.

Then there was a bump coming off of Turn 2, followed by a shimmy on the backstretch. Still, Dale thought he could hang on for one more mile. That's when the right rear tire exploded.

As the black No. 3 Chevy Lumina wobbled up the banking, Derrike Cope dived low and into the lead. Split seconds later, he took the checkered flag that was supposed to be Dale Earnhardt's.

A few days later, home in Welcome, North Carolina, Richard Childress took the slashed Goodyear tire from the No. 3 car that had just won the Daytona 499½ and nailed it over the door of the race shop. Another shot at that last half-mile was 364 days away.

FEB 25 1990

A half-inch. A measly half-inch. On a horribly cold day in Richmond at the Pontiac Excitement 400, that was the difference between celebration of the second win of Mark Martin's still-young career and embarrassment bordering on disgrace.

As Martin bantered with the media, his No. 6 Ford underwent its routine postrace inspection. That's when the half-inch made its presence known: an aluminum spacer placed beneath the carburetor, that measured 2.5 inches thick. The legal limit: two inches.

The victory stood, but officials socked Martin with a $40,000 fine and docked 46 points from his Winston Cup total.

Inspectors contended that the extra half-inch had allowed more air into the engine, creating a tiny bit more horsepower. Martin's employer, Roush Racing, claimed that the rigging was an honest mistake, and that anyway, there had been no performance advantage.

Nine months later, Dale Earnhardt won his fourth Winston Cup title. Martin finished second, 26 points behind. Without the penalty back in Richmond, he would have won the title by 20. Instead, he lost it by a lousy half-in-

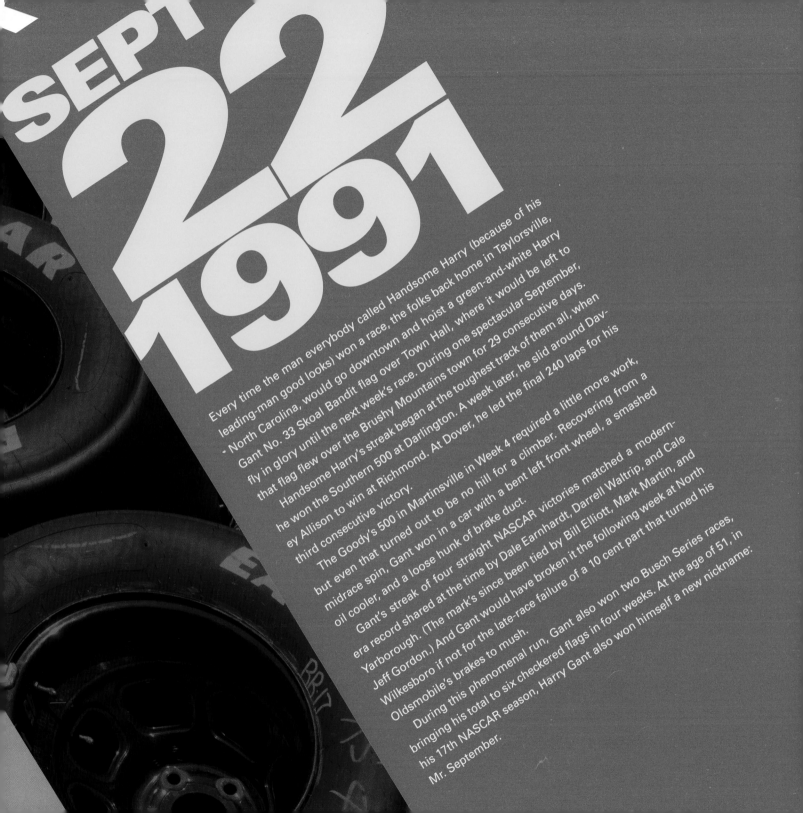

SEPT 22 1991

Every time the man everybody called Handsome Harry (because of his leading-man good looks) won a race, the folks back home in Taylorsville, North Carolina, would go downtown and hoist a green-and-white Harry Gant No. 33 Skoal Bandit flag over Town Hall, where it would be left to fly in glory until the next week's race. During one spectacular September, that flag flew over the Brushy Mountains town for 29 consecutive days.

Handsome Harry's streak began at the toughest track of them all, when he won the Southern 500 at Darlington. A week later, he slid around Davey Allison to win at Richmond. At Dover, he led the final 240 laps for his third consecutive victory.

The Goody's 500 in Martinsville in Week 4 required a little more work, but even that turned out to be no hill for a climber. Recovering from a midrace spin, Gant won in a car with a bent left front wheel, a smashed oil cooler, and a loose hunk of brake duct.

Gant's streak of four straight NASCAR victories matched a modern-era record shared at the time by Dale Earnhardt, Darrell Waltrip, and Cale Yarborough. (The mark's since been tied by Bill Elliott, Mark Martin, and Jeff Gordon.) And Gant would have broken it the following week at North Wilkesboro if not for the late-race failure of a 10 cent part that turned his Oldsmobile's brakes to mush.

During this phenomenal run, Gant also won two Busch Series races, bringing his total to six checkered flags in four weeks. At the age of 51, in his 17th NASCAR season, Harry Gant also won himself a new nickname: Mr. September.

T NIGHT

Humpy Wheeler was at it again.

As NASCAR marched its way onto the national stage, Wheeler knew that his sport's best shot at winning over new fans was to conjure up the spirits of its short-track roots. How about an old-school race under the lights on a Saturday night ... but on a 170 mph speedway?

"It goes back to primitive man," Wheeler explains. "Back then, greater alertness at night often meant the difference between life and death. Animal behavior is certainly different in the dark. Sharks, tigers, lions, and other big cats hunt primarily at night. Racers are no different."

So he wrapped his Charlotte Motor Speedway with more than 1,800 light fixtures, bathing the 1.5-mile track with 175 foot-candles of illumination. When the green flag dropped on what Wheeler billed as "One Hot Night," the primitives came out to play.

With one lap remaining, Dale Earnhardt led the race, tracked hard by Kyle Petty and Davey Allison. Petty shot down low to pass, Earnhardt dived to block, and just like that the No. 3 Chevy was spinning out of control and out of contention.

Now the sons of Richard and Bobby rocketed toward the finish line. In a final flash, Allison hemmed his way inside and won the side-by-side sprint to the finish line by inches. It was a win he wouldn't remember.

Just as the two cars took the checkered flag, Petty tapped Davey, sending his car around and into the wall with a spark-producing impact.

As his team gathered carless in Victory Lane, Allison lay strapped into a chopper overhead on his way to the hospital. The next day he would laugh about the win, the wreck, and the black hole in his memory.

But the moment had changed his life.

THE KING, THE KID, AND THE CUP
NOVEMBER 15,

As the 1992 season-capping Hooters 500 reached its halfway point, Benny Parsons—retired from the cockpit and in the broadcast booth for ESPN—conveyed to his audience the precise mood of everyone at the Atlanta Motor Speedway: "Folks, there's too much going on down there. It's too much for my brain to comprehend."

Six men had come to Atlanta with a mathematical chance of winning the Winston Cup title, but in reality, it was a three-car race.

Points leader Davey Allison was cruising toward the Cup when he wiped out with a little over 100 miles to go. That left it a two-man showdown: hometown hero Bill Elliott vs. stubborn, independent, and Wisconsin-born Alan Kulwicki.

Elliott won the race and led 102 laps. Kulwicki finished second but led 103. That extra lap earned him five bonus points for having led the most circuits on the day and clinched the Cup title by a record-low 10 points.

As the two men celebrated, one with a race-winner's trophy and the other with a Winston Cup, they both noticed that the crowd was paying them no attention. Instead, a track-shaking ovation was being directed at a wrecked race car taking one last lap at no more than 40 mph.

The fans were cheering for Richard Petty, 55, who had crashed his car earlier. The King was ending his 1,185th race in 35th place. There would be no 1,186th race.

Finishing four spots ahead of The King was Jeff Gordon, a.k.a. The Kid, whose first career start had gone pretty much like Petty's last: a midrace wreck and a back-of-the-pack finish overshadowed by the title bout.

Hail to The King! Hail to The Kid!

992

FATHER KNOWS BEST

People still don't believe Ned Jarrett when he tells the story. There's no way his son couldn't hear the coaching. No way.

Growing up, Dale Jarrett had seemed to lean more toward stick-and-ball sports than cars. But when Dale turned down a golf scholarship to the University of South Carolina, Ned concluded that his son must be serious about racing. Really serious.

And so in 1992, Dale crawled behind the wheel for new NASCAR owner Joe Gibbs. (Yep, the one with three Super Bowl rings.)

On Valentine's Day, Dale was running second in the Daytona 500 with two laps to go. Ned was in the broadcast booth, his foot tap-tap-tapping as he struggled to stay impartial and not jabber over play-by-play man Ken Squier. Then the call came into his headset from the CBS Sports producers: "Take it, Ned. Be a daddy."

Through the TV audience, Ned told Dale to get in behind Earnhardt, shake him loose, and take the lead. Dale did exactly that. Ned told Dale to get to the bottom of the track, protect that lead. Dale obeyed. Every time Ned suggested a maneuver, Dale obliged.

Final stop: Victory Lane.

When TV cameras spotted Martha Jarrett (the winner's mother) rocking and crying, Ned had one last command: "Somebody get down there and check on that girl. She needs help!"

"To this day, people swear Dale must have been able to hear what I was saying," Ned explains, smiling like a proud poppa. "He couldn't, of course. It was just instinct. Dale did what he needed to do."

The son leaned on a lifetime of fatherly advice.

Dale Jarrett, c. 1991.

The news crackled through the CB network linking a convoy of 18-wheelers crawling through the mountains that connect Tennessee, Virginia, and North Carolina. Each rig was owned by a Winston Cup team, packed with race cars and equipment, and headed toward the Bristol Motor Speedway. Now they were sharing some very bad news.

A plane had gone down around 9:30 p.m. somewhere near the Tri-Cities Airport in the Bristol area, a Merlin twin-engine turboprop registered to someone—nobody was sure to whom—in racing. The radios hummed with educated guesses (and borderline wild speculations) as team truckers silently prayed it hadn't been their driver.

Soon the truth was known: The defending Winston Cup champion was dead.

APRIL 1, 1993
A CHAMP'S FINAL FLIGHT

Alan Kulwicki and three others—two Hooters executives and the pilot—had been en route from an autograph session in Knoxville when they crashed just six miles from the airport. There were no survivors. Kulwicki was a headstrong independent who hadn't made many friends in NASCAR, but the way he had single-handedly willed his team to the title the season before had earned him the respect of everyone within the sport.

Three days later, Kulwicki's old Midwest short track rival Rusty Wallace won the Food City 500, after which he drove around the track clockwise—and backward.

That was exactly what Kulwicki had done at Atlanta five months earlier, when he had wrapped up the Winston title. Then, an exuberant Kulwicki had dubbed the stunt his "Polish victory lap." Today, Wallace saluted his friend in a manner befitting the man who had invented the move.

Suddenly, the sport and the men within it felt empty, vulnerable, and sick to their stomachs. As the series rolled forward into 1993, those feelings would only worsen.

TALLADEGA

All hell was going to break loose. How could it not? Rain forced a red flag stoppage in the action at the Winston 500 in Talladega, leaving 29 drivers to sit in their cars simmering and stewing, waiting for a restart. When the green flag was dropped, only two laps remained. Two laps at 190 mph, with 15 of those drivers believing they could win the race.

When the final lap started, Ernie Irvan was running fourth. Irvan had come east several years earlier—knocking on doors, sleeping in his truck—and built his own car. On this day, he drove like a man who wasn't going to be denied, slicing below Dale Earnhardt, Rusty Wallace, and Mark Martin to take the lead in Turn 1.

Earnhardt lost momentum and faded to ninth, then made a late

charge back toward the top five. To get there, he had to go through Wallace. The No. 3 Chevy hit the No. 2 Pontiac in the left rear bumper, and Wallace's sideways slide turned his car into an airplane wing. Rusty's vehicle sailed skyward, then nosed over into the asphalt, where it exploded in a series of flips stretching more than a half-mile that sent sheet metal and dirt flying in every direction.

Rusty sailed over the finish line in sixth place, behind winner Irvan and fourth-place finisher Earnhardt. Wallace suffered a broken wrist, a concussion, and a chipped tooth. A day later, he walked out of the hospital with his eyes swollen, his face bruised—and, because of the love tap from the No. 3 car that triggered all that damage, his relationship with Earnhardt forever injured.

THE END OF THE ALABAMA GANG

JULY 13, 1993

Since Davey Allison's wreck in the 1992 All-Star race, Liz Allison had noticed a change in her husband. Racing was no longer Davey's entire life. He was at home more, trying to be a part of his family's lives. "We became partners," she says. "We sort of became one."

When Bobby was hurt in 1988, Davey became family head and chief of the Alabama Gang, the band of racers who hailed from his hometown of Hueytown. Those roles were reinforced in the summer of 1992 when little brother Clifford was killed in a race car in Michigan.

On a midsummer Monday afternoon, Davey took off for Talladega in his new helicopter with old friend and Gang founder Red Farmer riding shotgun. Their mission was to watch Neil Bonnett's son, David, hit the big track for a test session. Davey believed that someday David would take Clifford's place by his side, just as the elder Bonnett had stood by Davey's dad.

Allison had owned the Hughes 369HS just a month, and he'd had only 10 hours of time at the stick. Suddenly, the chopper lurched out of control a few feet above the landing area then crashed. By the time it came to rest, Farmer had a broken collarbone, nose, and ribs. Davey Allison, 32, was dead.

At the funeral, Bobby hugged every neck he could find. Both of his boys were now gone. He and brother Donnie were crippled. At least, the old man admits having thought to himself at the time, the Bonnetts are still doing pretty good.

FEBRUARY 11, 1994

Neil Bonnett had always been close to the Allisons. Neil had sat with Davey when his uncle Donnie was hospitalized in 1981, when his father, Bobby, was hospitalized in 1988, and during his brother Clifford's funeral in 1992. A year later, it was Bonnett who pulled Davey Allison from the chopper wreckage at Talladega.

That grim day seemed to trigger something in Neil. A need to blot out horrible images? Or maybe just an old itch that needed scratching? Whatever it was, Bonnett quit his job as a TV analyst and got back behind the wheel.

Old buddy Dale Earnhardt put Bonnett in a couple of "R & D" rides in the months following Allison's death. And when the 1994 season started, Bonnett was a full-time racer for the first time in four years. The stories, the smiles, and the good times were back.

They lasted less than one practice session. Between Turns 3 and 4 at Daytona, Bonnett was killed in a crash, probably caused by a blown tire.

Three of NASCAR's biggest superstars—Alan Kulwicki, Davey Allison, Neil Bonnett— had died in less than 11 months. Now the sport looked to a pair of men to raise it from sadness, two rivals who could carry the sport to new heights—and into the next century.

AUGUST 6, 1994
ANOTHER BRICK IN THE WALL

In the early 1950s, Bill France Sr. took a trip to Indianapolis to see whether the Indy 500 lived up to all its hype and hoopla. When Indianapolis Motor Speedway owner Tony Hulman learned of his visitor's presence, he had France led off the property. Legend holds that Big Bill's parting words were, "Someday I'll own this place!" In fact, France merely figured he'd bring his cars up there when the time was right.

Four decades later, Hulman's grandson, Tony George, and France's son, Bill Jr., concluded that the time had finally arrived.

Open-wheel purists cried blasphemy. But when the gates were flung open for the inaugural Brickyard 400, 70 teams came seeking one of the race's 43 starting positions, and more than 350,000 tickets had been sold.

With four laps to go, leader Ernie Irvan felt his Ford wobble on Turn 1. The massive crowd came to its feet as Jeff Gordon, who had graduated from a high school only 20 miles down the road, made his move. The No. 24 Chevy grabbed the bottom groove and the lead as Irvan struggled to hang on to a rapidly deflating right front tire.

Two days earlier, Gordon had celebrated his 23rd birthday. Now he was being hailed as the first man to win at the Brickyard in a stock car.

When Richard Petty notched his seventh Winston Cup title in 1979, it was a record widely regarded as NASCAR's version of DiMaggio's hit streak or Wilt Chamberlain's 100-point game: unreachable. After all, no other driver had won more than three, and no heir apparent was on the horizon.

That same season, Dale Earnhardt won Rookie of the Year. But while The King was a clean-cut media dream, Ralph's kid was an unkempt mess. He couldn't handle himself with the press, couldn't keep a marriage together, and couldn't keep a race car in one piece. Petty was leader of the haves. Earnhardt lived among the have-nots.

But now, only 15 years later, on a chilly day at Rockingham in the Carolina Sandhills, Earnhardt became Petty's equal. He beat the AC-Delco 500 field into submission, leading the most laps, earning the 63rd win of his career, and clinching the coveted seventh Cup with two races remaining in the season.

"Not in my wildest dreams did I ever think I'd be here," The Intimidator told reporters, momentarily becoming that rough-ass, wide-eyed kid once again. "But let's get one thing straight: Richard Petty is still The King. I'm just happy to be mentioned with him."

1994

When Sterling Marlin's father, Coo Coo, decided it was time to put his teenage son behind the wheel of a Winston Cup car, he knew that his hardest job would be breaking the news to Sterling's mother. So the Nashville short-track legend slipped it in as matter-of-factly as he knew how: at the dinner table.

"Pass the potatoes, Eula Faye," Coo Coo said to his wife. "Sterling's racing this weekend at Talladega."

Nearly 20 years later, Sterling Marlin received another nugget of startling information in almost as casual a manner. This time, the news was delivered via radio by his crew chief, Tony Glover.

"You better go. He's comin'."

"He" was Dale Earnhardt. Marlin was leading the Daytona 500 with less than five laps to go, and Earnhardt was cutting his way up through the field thanks to four fresh tires after a yellow flag. When the race restarted, 11 laps remained, and The Intimidator was 14th. With one to go, he was glued to Marlin's back bumper. Dale's Daytona 500 winless streak was up to 16, but Marlin could have cared less, calmly moving his Kodak Chevy up and down the track to block No. 3's advance.

As the race ended, Marlin was the 500 champion for the second straight season. Earnhardt moved to 0-for-17.

"I still haven't won the damn Daytona 500," Earnhardt exclaimed as he exited his third runner-up ride. "And I ain't going to no damn Disney World, either!"

YO BE GO

THE ICEMAN WINNETH

If Dale Earnhardt was a chain saw, then Terry Labonte was a termite. One achieved greatness by destroying everything in his path, the other by quietly gnawing away.

Under the lights of Thunder Valley in Bristol, their different approaches had never been more obvious. Earnhardt bullied his way through the Goody 500 field for 500 laps, spinning Rusty Wallace early on and drawing a penalty. Labonte, meanwhile, hung near the front but didn't cause any commotion when he finally took the lead.

With a lap to go, Earnhardt had forced his way up to sit within inches of his old rival. As the two cars neared the finish line, The Intimidator gave the Iceman a shot, forcing the No. 5 Chevy into a wild, careening lunge toward the checkered flag. Labonte took the victory sideways, crossing the line and slamming into the wall just past the flag stand.

When Earnhardt pulled into the garage, Wallace was waiting. Wallace screamed, Dale smirked, and they went at it. As the two were separated, Wallace brought up Talladega 1993 and nailed Earnhardt in the noggin with a water bottle.

Meanwhile, Labonte pulled his mangled race car into Victory Lane. The crowd expected anger over the way the race had finished, but Texas Terry simply climbed out and shrugged his shoulders.

"Let the others do the yellin'," he said with a tight-lipped grin. "I'll take the win."

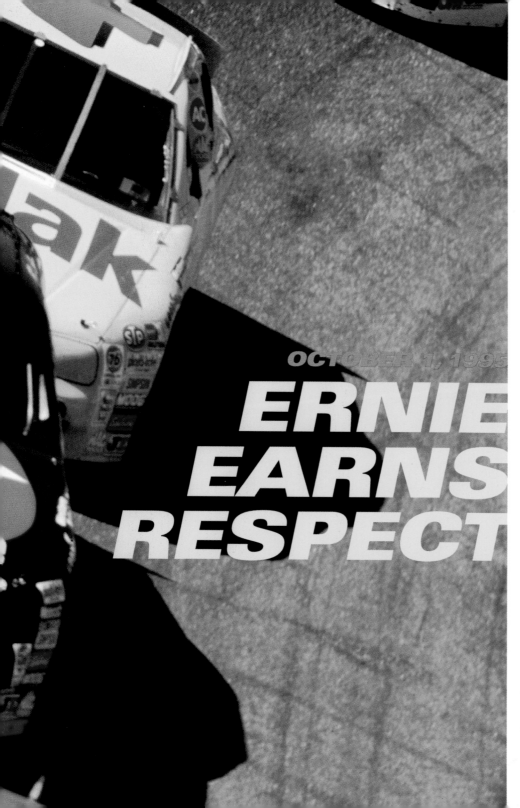

OCTOBER 1, 1995

ERNIE EARNS RESPECT

Ernie Irvan's life in Winston Cup had never been easy. His reckless reputation as Swervin' Irvan had dogged him so badly that he actually started a 1991 race weekend at Talladega by standing up in the prerace driver's meeting and apologizing for his wild style. It helped some, but earning the respect of his competition still seemed a hopeless challenge.

On Aug. 20, 1994, Irvan was a title contender. He'd replaced Davey Allison in Robert Yates' No. 28 Ford Thunderbird and sat second in points behind Dale Earnhardt. But a practice crash at Michigan nearly killed him; an emergency tracheotomy saved him as he sat dying against the Turn 2 wall.

Over the next year, Irvan survived a coma, pneumonia, swelling of the brain, and an aneurysm. But he reconditioned his body physically and mentally, motivated by the sole purpose of racing again.

One year, one month, and 11 days after his accident, Swervin' Irvan did just that, competing at the North Wilkesboro Speedway, first in a NASCAR Truck Series event, then a Winston Cup race, the Tyson Holly Farms 400. He led for a while in both, and finished sixth on Sunday.

Sure, there were whispers about his eye patch, rumors about his seeing double, about his having vertigo at high speeds. But Ernie Irvan had lived with accusatory chatter of one sort or another his entire career.

None of that mattered. He was alive, he was racing, and he was back up front.

As Jeff Gordon gobbled up more wins and Cup points, he began to notice a new element in the noise ringing in his ears at the track: boos.

When Gordon first showed up at the track, the fans didn't think much of who he was and where he came from. So what if he was born in California, came from open-wheel racing, had neatly coiffed hair. So what if he didn't hunt or fish, didn't have a Southern accent, and drove a race car painted the colors of the rainbow.

None of that worked against him until he started to win.

How dare he win more races than Dale Earnhardt! How could he allow himself to stand in the way of Dale's eighth championship? And what was with that hair, anyway?

When the checkered flag came down on the 1995 season in Atlanta at the NAPA 500, The Intimidator was standing in Victory Lane celebrating one of the most dominating wins of his career. But The Kid won the Cup, boos and all, by 34 points.

The sport's next great rivalry, one to be fought more in the grandstand than on the racetrack, was now officially underway.

NOV 12 1995

THE KID BECOMES THE MAN

MONTE CARLO

MAN... OR

JULY 26, 1996

All was right in the universe once again. Midway through the 1996 season, Dale Earnhardt was only a dozen points out of the championship lead and, with a dozen laps to go at the DieHard 500 in Talladega, The Intimidator was in position to seize that lead with a victory.

Ernie Irvan was tucked in close behind Earnhardt, while Sterling Marlin rode to their outsides. Irvan, misjudging Marlin's position, moved up the track, made contact, and knocked Marlin sideways. The No. 4 Kodak Chevy hit Earnhardt's No. 3 car and sent it directly into the frontstretch wall at nearly 200 mph. The black Monte Carlo slid on its driver's-side window before being flipped into the air by a crushing rooftop blow from the onrushing car of Robert Pressley.

The Intimidator had long situated his racing seat lower than most, believing it helped him maintain a better feel for the mood of his race cars. On this day, that low-slung position saved his life, keeping his head well below the point of contact with Pressley's vehicle.

Dale's collarbone was broken and his sternum cracked. For the first time in nearly 15 seasons, the most bulletproof man in NASCAR history had been physically hurt. The lingering pain would eventually alter his livelihood, his life, and his legacy.

SUPERMAN?

AUGUST 9, 1996

Dale Earnhardt promised to get out of the car. He promised his wife, Teresa. He promised his race team. And he promised his car owner, Richard Childress.

Earnhardt promised to do what he had done at Indianapolis a week earlier, the week following his Talladega crash: take the green flag to earn the day's points in The Glen at Watkins Glen, then climb out of the car under the first caution period, put a relief driver behind the wheel, and repair to

an easy chair to let his injuries heal.

Forget the hit his pride had taken when he'd climbed out of the No. 3 Chevy at Indy, forfeiting a chance to defend his Brickyard 400 title.

Forget that he'd somehow won the pole position on Friday, wincing his way around the Watkins Glen road course with a torso full of broken bones.

Forget all that. He'd promised everyone that he'd get out of the car, hadn't he?

Promises, promises.

Earnhardt grimaced through the pain to lead the race's first 29 laps. He led twice more for a total of 54 circuits, more than half the event and the most of any driver on the day. In the end, he faded to what was still a logic-bending sixth-place finish, then slid gingerly out of his race car, trying not to favor his left shoulder.

Trying to ignore his broken promises.

The legend of The Intimidator had gained another chapter, though the price paid to write it would prove to be costly.

TRIPLE PLAY FEBRO

Jeff Gordon won the 1995 championship, followed by teammate Terry Labonte in 1996. A decade after rolling the dice on NASCAR, Hendrick Motorsports had turned itself into a dynasty.

But during the winter of 1996, the party suddenly came to a screeching halt. Team owner Rick Hendrick was indicted for activities involving his auto sales empire, followed by news that, at age 47, he had leukemia. When his teams arrived in Daytona to start the 1997 season, their boss wasn't in attendance, but the emotions stirred by his absence were converted into horsepower.

With 11 laps left, Dale Earnhardt brought out the caution with a bizarre backstretch crash. His car flipped but came to rest on its wheels, allowing The Intimidator to drive off with some pride after yet another Daytona 500 failure.

On the final restart, Bill Elliott led, but with a mirror full of Hendrick race cars. Gordon dove low; Labonte climbed high. Elliott hesitated on whom he should block and ended up stopping no one. Gordon took the checkered flag, Labonte came in second, and Ricky Craven—in a Hendrick Chevy—rocketed past Elliott to take third.

In Victory Lane, all three Hendrick Motorsports drivers celebrated. For the first time all winter, the teammates could finally smile, able to throw the victory party that had been stolen from them in December.

ARY 16, 1997

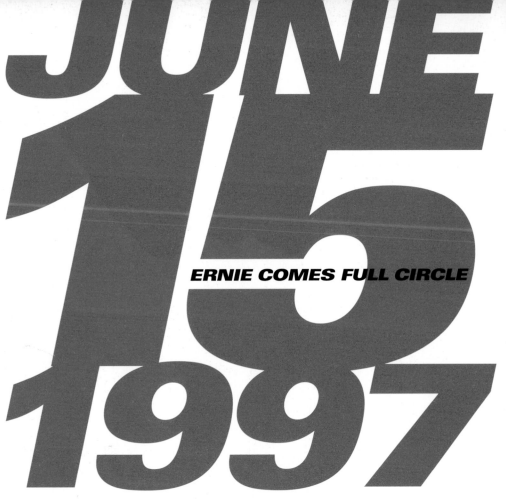

JUNE 15 1997

ERNIE COMES FULL CIRCLE

Ernie Irvan's return to Robert Yates Racing was bittersweet. He was happy to be back, but wary of working with Dale Jarrett, the man who had replaced him after his near-fatal crash in 1994.

Irvan had gone from No. 1 driver at RYR to second chair. He'd won two races since his comeback, but Dale always seemed to accomplish more. In 1996, Jarrett finished third in the point standings and won five races, including the Daytona 500. By June 1997, DJ had already won twice and was on the pole for the Miller 400 in Brooklyn, Michigan.

Irvan sensed he'd be bumped by RYR at season's end. But before then, doggone it, he would finally conquer the track that had nearly killed him.

Two hundred times Ernie blasted by the Turn 2 wall where he'd once sat covered in blood, and 200 times he never flinched. The victory was the 15th and final of Irvan's career, which ended two years later after a practice crash at—where else?—Michigan.

Something had
to happen, right? A cut tire,
a pinched fuel line, a bad pit stop—hell,
a meteorite blowing a hole into the backstretch, *something*. Why not? After all,
it always did when Dale Earnhardt hit the
asphalt at the Daytona 500.

Yet here was The Intimidator, once again
leading the Great American Race during its
final stanza. Nineteen times he had gone
south to Daytona, and 19 times he'd gone
back to North Carolina with nothing but
a clenched, pride-biting smile. Fourteen
times he'd finished in the top 10, including
three runners-up over his latest five tries.

So with two laps to go, with Dale running up front and a pack of cars nipping at

his spoiler,
something had to
give. The crowd, eerily silent,
waited for it. Pit Road, which included
many rivals who were secretly rooting for
him to win, waited for it.

Then, as if God himself couldn't take it
any longer, there was a crash behind him
off Turn 2, essentially ending the race one
lap early. Dale Earnhardt, his generation's
greatest racer, had finally won his sport's
greatest event.

When Dale first came to Daytona, back

in 1979, he
was 27 years old,
nearly homeless, and aching
for respect. Two decades, seven championships, and 71 wins later, the entire NASCAR
community lined up to produce a half-mile-
long line of congratulatory high fives.

It was only the single greatest display of
respect in NASCAR history.

Every weekend during the 1998 season, NASCAR found different ways to celebrate its 50th anniversary. It recognized its 50 greatest drivers, owners, and mechanics. It brought legends like Petty, Pearson, and Yarborough out to the track to tell stories about the all-time greatest stock car seasons. But truth is, if fans wanted a history lesson, they needed only marvel at what was taking place right in front of them.

Jeff Gordon, backed by crew chief Ray Evernham and his Rainbow Warrior pit crew, put on a show in 1998 the likes of which may never be seen again. In 33 tries, Gordon won 13 times, matching Richard Petty's modern-era record. He finished inside the top 10 an astonishing 28 times—and 26 times in the top five or better. His average finish for the entire season was 5.7, boosted by a record-tying four-race win streak, a stretch that included his fourth consecutive Southern 500 at Darlington.

"If he does nothing else in his career," said Darrell Waltrip, "that's enough to be ranked as an all-time great."

Gordon closed out the year with a romp at the NAPA 500 in Atlanta, leading 113 of 221 laps, for his 42nd win and third Cup championship in four seasons.

"Good drivers have great seasons," Waltrip proclaimed. "But the truly great drivers have eras. Ladies and gentlemen, this is the Jeff Gordon Era."

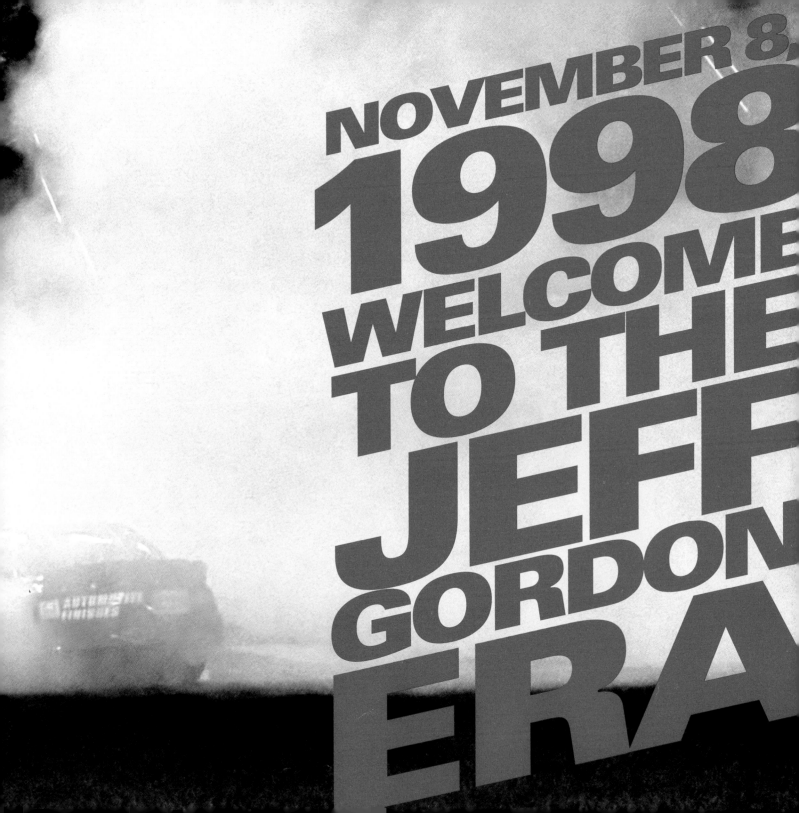

NOVEMBER 8,
1998
WELCOME
TO THE
JEFF
GORDON
ERA

RETURN OF THE INTIMIDATOR

AUGUST 28, 1999

For the first time in a long time, Dale Earnhardt felt good. Lingering injuries from his 1996 Talladega crash had slowed him down much more than his pride would let on. A "dream team" marriage with crew chief Larry McReynolds had resulted in the Daytona 500 win but little else. The biggest victory of Dale's career had ended up becoming the lone bright spot in a miserable 1-for-100 drought.

But now he felt good. He was eating better, he had lost a little weight, and he had let a doctor dig some floating bone chips out of his back. He won at Talladega in April, started making noise in the points standings, and more important, got his swagger back.

Here he was again, at Bristol, on the final lap of the Goody's 500 with Terry Labonte just off his front bumper. Four years earlier, he had waited until Turn 4 to put that bumper to his old hunting buddy, too late. This time, he used his chrome calling card a half lap earlier, sending Labonte around in a cloud of tire smoke and jetting by for the win.

As he raised his arms in victory, Earnhardt was washed with a wave of sound he hadn't heard since his dirt-track days.

The crowd booed the hell out of him.

The Intimidator's reaction was the same as it had been back in the day: He smiled.

"Hey," he said to his team, who were visibly shaken up by the reaction. "At least they're making noise."

CAR
ES
GE

For 10 years, every race on the NASCAR Winston Cup schedule had been televised. By 1999, every Busch and Truck Series event was being carried live, and even select practice and qualifying sessions were on the air. But a patchwork of broadcast deals struck individually from track to track was creating viewer confusion. Race coverage jumped channels on a near-weekly basis, leaving fans to wade through an alphabet soup of call letters and cable channels.

Bill France Jr. recognized the problem, with its attendant loss of potential revenue, and started shopping for an NFL-style television package to be negotiated centrally by the league itself. The result was a six-year, $2.4 billion agreement with FOX, NBC, Turner Sports, and TBS that split the season in half and kept the vast majority of Winston Cup races on old-fashioned, over-the-air network TV.

The first race covered by the new partners would be the 2001 Daytona 500. It would become the single greatest watershed moment in American motorsports history, but for a reason no one could have possibly predicted.

A casual stroll through the Winston Cup garage during the 2000 season would have revealed the changing face of the sport: younger, prettier, and, more often than not, without a Southern accent.

Jeff Gordon's success had rendered much of NASCAR's conventional criteria for scouting talent obsolete, forcing team owners and sponsors to rewrite the user's manual on what to look for in a driver. The average age behind the wheel began to plummet, from the fortysomethings of the 1990s to guys just old enough to buy beer. The Southeast was now merely another place to look for drivers, not the only place.

And in the nationwide talent search, experience now took a backseat to potential. The Midwest's sprint car pipeline produced Kenny Irwin, Tony Stewart, and Ryan Newman. From the heartland came the calculating minds of Carl Edwards and Matt Kenseth. And the West Coast, long an untapped region for speedsters, turned out an off-road racer named Jimmie Johnson and an all-star team of short-track aces, from Greg Biffle and Kevin Harvick to Kasey Kahne and the Busch brothers.

But the new millennium's earliest and flashiest headlines still belonged to the royal families of NASCAR, as the sport's two greatest surnames sired yet another generation of racers.

FULL SPEED AHEAD

MAY 12, 2000
A KINGDOM MOURNS

On April 2, 2000, 19-year-old Adam Petty made his Winston Cup debut in the DIRECTV 500 at the Texas Motor Speedway, becoming America's first fourth-generation pro athlete. The great-grandson of Lee and the grandson of Richard was stoked, but Adam's lifelong dream hadn't been to race with the big boys—it had been to race against his father, Kyle.

But Kyle Petty hadn't made the field, so he was watching his son's first NASCAR start from the pit. Then, a third of the way into the race, the Wood Brothers' team needed a driver to relieve an ailing Elliott Sadler. So Kyle strapped himself into the No. 21 car and went roaring onto the track ... just as Adam's Chevy limped out of the race with a blown motor.

"I thought my dream was going to come true there for a minute," Adam said with a grimace. "But we'll get another chance."

Three days later, Kyle's phone rang. Bad news: Lee Petty had died at the age of 86, having fought off the effects of a stomach aneurysm just long enough to see his great-grandson race on TV.

Five weeks later, Kyle got another phone call, this one with even worse news. During a practice run before a Busch Series race in Loudon, New Hampshire, the throttle on son Adam's Chevy had frozen. Adam hit the Turn 3 wall at high speed. He had died instantly.

Fifty-two NASCAR seasons separated the debuts of Lee and Adam Petty. They died only 37 days apart. Between them spread the greatest family legacy in sports.

Now, for the first time, the Kingdom was without an heir.

OCTOBER 25, 2000
SEE THE AIR,
BE THE AIR

Only one thing could explain how Dale Earnhardt piled up top-five finishes on the perilous high banks of Daytona and Talladega with maneuvers mere mortals could never even approach.

The Intimidator could see the air.

Earnhardt politely denied having supernatural powers, claiming that his success on the two ovals resulted from experience, a trained eye, a finely honed sense of anticipation, a great crew, and … blah blah blah.

His fellow competitors weren't buying it. They knew there had to be something else going on.

Take, for instance, the 2000 Winston 500 at Talladega. When the lead pack crossed the start-finish line with three laps to go, Earnhardt was way back in 18th place, wedged in the middle of a three-wide freight train with nowhere to go. That's when he spotted Kenny Wallace, little brother of Rusty, on his back bumper. Dale curled a finger to signal, "Come on, let's go."

And off they went.

The two cars acted as one, darting past one car and then another until they returned to the flag stand, by which time No. 3 had moved inside the top 10. Then, as they took

the one-lap-to-go signal, Earnhardt suddenly gunned into the lead, and an electrified crowd roared over the stampede of engines below.

For the 76th time in his career, Dale Earnhardt pulled into Victory Lane. Back in the garage, rivals climbed from their cars, looked at one another, and started laughing. What else could they do?

"You see something like that," said Dale Jarrett, who finished 15th, "and it makes you want to go out to the souvenir stands and buy one of his damned T-shirts. Tell he can't see the air? Sure he can."

FEBRUARY 18, 2001
DEATH OF A LEGEND

In the days leading up to his 23rd Daytona 500, Dale Earnhardt shared the same dec-
laration with anyone who would listen: "I've got it all, man! I really do have it all."

The seven-time Cup champion was 49 going on 29. His third marriage was a
wall-to-wall success. He'd mended fences with his enemies. He'd grown closer to
his family. And he'd finished second in the 2000 season points standings. What's
more, he was now a team owner, with three cars in the field being driven by hand-
picked protégé Steve Park; Darrell Waltrip's little brother, Michael; and his son,
Dale Earnhardt Jr.

Flash forward to one lap to go in the Great American Race. The Intimidator was
playing The Defender, shamelessly blocking all the cars behind him, keeping them
herded behind his back bumper. Why? Because the two cars up front were his cars.

That's right: Michael Waltrip and Junior were running 1-2, and by God, Dale was
going to make sure they finished that way.

But suddenly, the unthinkable happened.

Between Turns 3 and 4, Earnhardt took a shot from somebody who was trying
to edge past him. The No. 3 car wobbled left, then darted up the track and into the
wall at the top of Turn 4 in the middle of a multicar crackup.

Dale Earnhardt died instantly, killed in the final turn of NASCAR's biggest race,
in front of its largest-ever television audience.

The blow staggered NASCAR like no other, and it had absorbed many over the
decades. Not that of Little Joe. Nor Fireball. Not even of Alan and Davey.

To NASCAR, Dale Earnhardt was Elvis … John Lennon … JFK.

Once the initial shock wore off, everyone agreed that his death marked the end
of an era.

What no one could possibly know, what no one could even imagine, was that
The Intimidator's impact on the sport he loved was only just beginning.

.06 SECONDS

MARCH 11, 2001

20 INCHES

FADE TO WHITE

In the days following the death of his best friend, Richard Childress thought long and hard about closing up shop.

But he pushed through the pain, as he knew Dale would have insisted he do. Between memorial services and receiving lines, Childress told the team to paint the GM Goodwrench Chevy white, find an available number, and get ready to go racing.

Kevin Harvick, a 25-year-old who had never started a Winston Cup race, took the wheel. At Rockingham, he finished 14th (Steve Park won in a Dale Earnhardt, Incorporated car). And in Las Vegas, Harvick celebrated an eighth-place effort by getting married two days later.

Now, Harvick held the lead with one lap to go in the Cracker Barrel 500 in Atlanta. He rode high along the wall in Turn 4 and cut back hard toward the finish. Beneath him, Jeff Gordon, pulled alongside at 190 mph. The two set out on a drag race to the finish line.

"It's Harvick!" play-by-play man Mike Joy yelled through tears in the TV booth. "Harvick by inches!" (Exactly 20 of them, if you're scoring at home.)

Dale's car had won, by all of .006 seconds, in the second-closest finish since NASCAR had installed its computerized system.

The closest? A .005-second win by Earnhardt himself, over Ernie Irvan at Talladega in 1993.

ONE FOR THE SON
JULY 7, 2001

Steve Park's win at Rockingham one week after Earnhardt's death had gone a long way toward helping the shattered Dale Earnhardt, Incorporated team begin the healing process. Harvick's victory two weeks later had done the same for Richard Childress Racing.

Healing rituals took place at every racetrack every weekend into the summer, as fans bonded at memorial services and candlelight vigils, and even started flashing a three-finger salute during the third lap of races.

Dale Jr., however, was not healing as quickly. The constant cycle of well wishes and outpoured emotions, while appreciated, ripped his wounded heart open again every day. He dragged his way through spring and early summer, sleepwalking through his grief.

When it came time to return to Daytona in July for the Pepsi 400, he drove into the track early, walked up onto the banking, and sat down on the spot off the track where his father had last been alive. He made his peace with the old speedway, but not before vowing to break its neck.

Under the lights and the microscope, Dale Jr. delivered the kind of comeback that only his bloodline could produce, roaring from sixth to first in the closing laps to take the victory.

Then, standing on top of his car, his arms stretched toward the heavens, he did something he hadn't been able to do in nearly five months.

Dale Earnhardt Jr. smiled—and in so doing went from a boy to a man before NASCAR Nation's very eyes.

AUGUST 21, 2001

Before the start of the 2001 season, Dale Earnhardt had called the NASCAR offices in Daytona and offered to help promote this, the most pivotal of racing years. The new television deal was in place, two new tracks were open for business, and the seven-time champ had wanted to help the league capitalize on the certain wave of new fans.

He died before he could become NASCAR's premier PR man. But in a twisted way, his death brought more eyes to the sport than anything he could have done while alive. He put NASCAR on the cover of *Time*, on the front page of *The Wall Street Journal*, and before bulging TV audiences every week.

All the attention forced NASCAR officials to deal with a tidal wave of questions about safety and the cause of The Intimidator's death, as well as those of three others since May 2000—Adam Petty, Kenny Irwin, and Truck Series driver Tony Roper.

Finally, the two-part "Official Accident Report, No. 3 Car" was unveiled in a Washington-style press conference. The autopsy, along with computer re-creations, reams of real-time data, and countless crash reenactments, determined that Earnhardt had been killed by blunt force trauma and a basal skull fracture, possibly the result of a torn lap belt.

Sweeping new safety changes accompanied the report: including the addition of on-site medical advisers and the formation of a new NASCAR Research and Development Center.

The highest-profile addition among the new rules—HANS—could very well have saved Dale Earnhardt's life, despite the fact that Earnhardt hated the equipment it called for.

RNHARDT IMPACT

OCTOBER 17, 2001
In the 1980s, Dr. Robert Hubbard, a Michigan State engineering professor, was chatting with his brother-in-law, road racer Jim Downing, about the recent death of a friend and fellow racer.

The friend, as well as all four NASCAR drivers killed in 2000-01, had succumbed to a basal skull fracture. When a vehicle hits a concrete wall at high speeds, it comes to a sudden stop. The driver's body, strapped into the race seat, stops with it, but the unrestrained head continues to move forward. The result is a likely separation of the head from the spinal cord, causing a spinal fracture and the potential for fatal trauma. Hubbard began to work on a device to limit the head's forward motion in the event of a crash, keeping head and body as one.

What Hubbard and his research team came up with was the HANS (Head and Neck Support) Device, a carbon-fiber shoulder harness that attaches to the torso and the helmet, keeping them connected.

At the start of the 2000 season, only one Winston Cup driver, Brett Bodine, used the HANS. Others, including Earnhardt, rejected the idea, citing restricted head movement and a potential hindrance to quick car exits in an emergency.

But Earnhardt's death had inspired a lot of the skeptics to conversion, and the last holdouts were being forced into line by a new, nonnegotiable NASCAR mandate.

"I think one day we will all look back and really be mad at ourselves," said Ricky Craven, himself a victim of multiple concussive hits in the 1990s.

"We'll ask, Why in the world did we wait so long to do something so obvious? Who could still be here if only we had acted just a little sooner?"

THE RETURN OF THE RAINBOW WARRIOR

Since Jeff Gordon had won the 1998 Winston Cup title, his star had cooled even though his burn to win had not. At the end of 1999, mentor and crew chief Ray Evernham left the No. 24 team to spearhead Dodge's return to NASCAR. Together, Evernham and Gordon had won three championships and 47 races, but like Richard Petty and Dale Inman two decades earlier, they longed to prove they could win apart.

In 2000, Gordon won "only" three times, finishing ninth in points and doing little to muffle the "Jeff can't do it without Ray" chatter. To find his footing, Gordon coaxed crew chief Robbie Loomis to leave a lifetime at Petty Enterprises and take charge of the Rainbow Warriors.

Evernham had redefined the modern-day crew chief, employing revolutionary strategies and an army of engineers. Loomis, given to spinning yarns about his days with The King and gnawing on bell peppers as if they were apples, was so old-school, he was damn near rustic. The new chief used his steady, old-fashioned ways to steer his team and driver through the Earnhardt tragedy, the resulting safety paranoia, and even 9/11 to score six wins, including their third Brickyard 500.

The pot of gold at the end of this new rainbow turned up at the NAPA 500 in Atlanta, where a sixth-place finish clinched Gordon's fourth Winston Cup, second only to Petty's and Earnhardt's seven.

Gordon expressed just one regret: "I didn't get to race Dale Earnhardt for it."

NOV 18 2001

TOO TOUGH TO TAME

On the eve of her 99th Winston Cup event, the Lady in Black was fighting for her life.

Since 1950, the Darlington Raceway had served as NASCAR's litmus test: If a driver won a race on this ribbon of sandpaper, it had little to do with aerodynamics or deep pockets. It ment he knew what to do when he slid behind the wheel of a race car.

But now the historic raceway was falling apart and falling behind. Slowly but surely, NASCAR expansion was killing the old Southern tracks in favor of larger, sexier, newer locales. North Wilkesboro was shuttered, Rockingham was on life support, and Darlington was on notice.

Prove your worth or get out of the way was the message Darlington heard loud and clear. So the old girl called on the legends of races past for help. She lit a candle to Johnny Mantz; conjured up the ghosts of Buck Baker and Curtis Turner, to inhabit the bodies of the youngsters who'd taken over the pack; and opened the gates for the Carolina Dodge Dealers 400.

What Darlington somehow succeeded in summoning up was her most scintillating showdown ever. For two laps—nearly three miles—24-year-old phenom Kurt Busch and 36-year-old vet Ricky Craven banged doors, at 170 mph. Busch hip-checked Craven on the frontstretch, and Craven replied by putting his opponent into the Turn 1 wall with such a bang that it nearly blew out a television microphone.

The pair roared fender to fender around the final turn, the one Harold Brasington had built extra tight so as not to disturb a popular local fishing hole. They swapped sheet metal once, twice, three times, and ultimately, both cars were sent smoking sideways across the stripe.

Craven was the winner by .002 seconds, a new standard for closest margin of victory. Astonished, the crowd formed a line to buy tickets for Darlington's next event … and the next … and the next.

The Track Too Tough to Tame was now the Track Too Tough to Terminate.

JUNE 19, 2003

In the three decades since 1971, R.J. Reynolds Tobacco had underwritten much of NASCAR's chart-busting growth. During that boom era, the company crowned 15 different Winston Cup champions and lined NASCAR pockets with plenty of cash. Smokes and hot cars—it seemed like the perfect marriage.

But as with so many unions these days, strains began to develop. RJR had gotten into racing as a way to bypass government advertising restrictions, and now, at the beginning of the new millennium, additional restrictions were lurking around the racetrack. Not only that, but NASCAR was beginning to feel uncomfortable about its very public connection to cigarettes.

So finally, despite all the good times, Big Tobacco and Big Racing decided to call it quits.

About that time NASCAR got a phone call …

Virginia-based Nextel Communications, pioneer of the push-to-talk mobile phone, was searching for a high-tech, high-speed vehicle to reach the masses. Three decades after Bill France Sr. had welcomed RJR with open arms, Bill Jr. formally ushered in the NASCAR Nextel Cup era with a 10-year sponsorship deal estimated to be worth $700 million.

"We will always be indebted to Winston for what they did for the sport," said four-time Winston Cup champion Jeff Gordon. "But as long as we were connected to cigarettes, there was going to be a stigma. The change in our image will be overnight."

Not to mention the size of their checking accounts.

SEPTEMBER 13, 2003

On Nov. 5, 1978, the Dixie 500 at the Atlanta International Raceway was in an uproar. Richard Petty was flagged the race winner, but Donnie Allison protested, claiming that he was the rightful victor, the victim of a scoring snafu.

As Bill France Jr. worked to calm teams and confer with officials, someone suggested that he might want to go up to the press box. It seems that his son, Brian, had called a press conference, eager to explain that Allison was indeed the winner and that he could prove it.

Brian France was 16 years old.

Like his father before him, Brian grew up in, around, even underneath the racetrack. Like both Bills, Brian put in his dues at the short tracks. He managed Saturday-night races, helped found the Truck Series, and along the way, sold everything from programs to tickets to nachos.

Now, at the age of 41, a quarter-century after his first "intervention" in a NASCAR event, Brian France was named chairman and CEO of the league—and caretaker of his grandfather's dream. Though he had orchestrated much of the Nextel deal behind the scenes, he had no problem letting his father bask in the glory of the lucrative package.

The next major announcement would be even bigger—a revolutionary alteration of the way championships were won.

And this one would be an idea that was all Brian.

JANUARY 20, 2004

The 2003 championship race was more of a mercy killing than a fight. Matt Kenseth routed the rest of the field with a relentless barrage of top-10 finishes, clinching the last of the Winston Cup titles a week before the year's final race.

For the fifth time in six years, the championship had been a runaway decided well before the end of the season.

NASCAR had always had to cope with an annual dip in television ratings when football season kicked off in the autumn; having the title already locked up simply made matters worse.

Brian France and his VP of licensing, Mark Dyer, both admitted football junkies, wrestled with the problem and came to the conclusion that racing needed a postseason, its own version of the playoff schemes that had been such a boon to baseball, pro football, and pro hoops.

Gentlemen, start your engines: The Chase for the Nextel Cup is on.

The way the Chase for the Nextel Cup works, France and Dyer explained, is that with 10 races remaining in the season, the top 10 drivers would enter the Chase. Essentially, they'd hit the reset button on the points standings, and the championship race would start anew, with 10 drivers going for the gold.

Traditionalists scoffed. Drivers expressed concern that more than three-quarters of the 43-man pack would be irrelevant each September. Sponsors fretted that the value of their investments would plummet if their cars were left out in the non-Chase cold.

Even Bill Jr., Brian's dad, had his doubts.

But Brian preached patience. Give it a try, he said. Let's see how it turns out. Wait until the end of the season to throw your darts.

By November, all that was being thrown at the Chase was praise.

Back in the day, Ralph Earnhardt roughhoused his way around the dirt tracks of the South with good friend and occasional partner Ralph Eury. In the pits, his son, Dale, hung out with Eury's son, Tony, and the two boys became lifelong friends and eventually brothers-in-law. Their marriages failed, but their sons—Dale Jr. and Tony Jr.—became close friends in their own right.

So when Dale Earnhardt began constructing the team that would support and surround his son, he looked no further than family. Tony Sr. called the shots, Tony Jr. turned the wrenches, and Dale Jr. turned the wheel.

They won on the short tracks of the Carolina Piedmont, followed by two Busch Series titles, and then scored nine wins in their first four Cup seasons. Along the way, they did what a family does: They argued, they threw tire irons in the garage, they kicked toolboxes, and they screamed over the radio that connected car and pit.

"I know some people think we're just crazy rednecks," Junior said in explanation. "But it works for us."

No kidding.

At the Daytona 500, just as they had been when Dale Jr.'s father was alive, all eyes were on an Earnhardt. While the Eurys calculated pit strategy, Dale Jr. led six times for 59 laps and outraced Tony Stewart to the line by less than three-tenths of a second.

It had taken Dale Sr. 20 years to win the Daytona 500. On the third anniversary of his dad's death, Dale Jr. won the Great American Race on only his fifth try.

FOLLOWING IN BIG FOOTPRINTS

SEPTEMBER 11, 2004

L—O—N—G SHOT

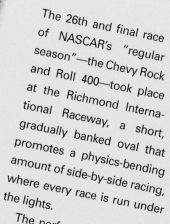

The 26th and final race of NASCAR's "regular season"—the Chevy Rock and Roll 400—took place at the Richmond International Raceway, a short, gradually banked oval that promotes a physics-bending amount of side-by-side racing, where every race is run under the lights.

The perfect track for a bunkhouse stampede.

Nine drivers had shots at the five remaining Chase positions. Of them, Jeremy Mayfield was the longest shot, four slots out of the coveted 10th place. He needed a perfect night: win the race and lead the most laps. A tall order for a driver who hadn't won since June 19, 2000, and was 0 for his last 21 at Richmond.

But a series of mishaps and mistakes scrambled the odds. Suddenly, with eight laps to go, crew chief Kenny Francis' voice crackled over the radio: "Mr. Mayfield, you are the freakin' leader of this freakin' race!"

Flash forward to the checkered flag. Mayfield earned five bonus points for leading a lap, five for leading the most laps, and five for winning, for a total of 15 points. He left Richmond a proud member of NASCAR's inaugural class of Chasers—by a margin of seven points.

NOVEMBER 21

VINDIC

1. KURT BUSCH
2. JIMMIE JOHN

Those few souls who had dared to stand with Brian France and buy into the idea of the Chase were gloating. The top five drivers came to the 2004 season finale separated by only 82 points. Kurt Busch led by 18 over Jimmie Johnson and by 21 over Johnson's teammate Jeff Gordon.

Through four hours of racing on the 1.5-

mile oval of Homestead-Miami in the Ford 400, the Roush Racing Ford and the Hendrick Chevys kept each other within striking distance, each taking a turn in the championship lead.

Nearing the race's halfway point, Busch narrowly avoided a wreck and then barely avoided crushing into the Pit Road wall when his right front tire came off its posts and

2004

ATION!

$$\frac{6,506 - 6,498}{8}$$

SON

turned his Taurus into a 3,400-pound tri-cycle. The mess left the 26-year-old in 28th place, but by the final lap, he was once again glued to the rear bumpers of Johnson and Gordon.

One last caution flag set up a final one-lap dash to determine the race and the title. Johnson and Gordon ran 2-3, taking shots at leader Greg Biffle, one of Busch's Roush

teammates. Meanwhile, Busch worked every mirror and corner of his peripheral vision, protecting his fifth-place position. The strategy worked: Biffle won the race, and Busch (who held on to fifth) won the Nextel Cup.

Busch's eight-point margin over Johnson and 16-point edge over Gordon easily made this the tightest title bout in more than half a century of NASCAR racing.

A few hours later, a NASCAR official ran from garage to garage, looking behind everything from tire stacks to template racks. What was he looking for? Someone to ask him that very question.

Finally someone bit, and he whipped out his ready-made answer:

"I'm looking for all those people who said this Chase deal wasn't going to work."

THE NEW OLD RIVALRY
FEBRUARY 20, 2005

After his father's death, Dale Earnhardt Jr. inherited The Intimidator's old-school fan base. Little E, now 30, had also inherited his father's last great rival, Jeff Gordon. But the rivalry actually lived more in the grandstand than on the racetrack, as few head-to-head moments had materialized.

Cue Daytona. The place where it all began stepped forward—as it so often had—to provide just such a magic moment.

You couldn't have predicted any magic in the 2005 Daytona 500 from the race's first 400 miles. For most of the day, there wasn't much all that great about the Great American Race. But then business started picking up.

Gordon ripped the lead away from Tony Stewart as the closing laps approached. For much of the race, Dale Jr. had struggled to control his race car, but now he was finally in the mix with Stewart, Gordon, Kurt Busch, and Jimmie Johnson. And that's when the old rivalry heated up.

Lap 198: Little E takes the lead, but a yellow caution flag—the record-tying 11th on the day—forces a reversion to the last scoring loop, which gives the lead back to Gordon. It also sets up another green-white-checkered scenario that will turn the race into the Daytona 507.5.

Lap 202: The green flag goes up, with Gordon, Dale Jr., Johnson, and Busch practically sharing paint.

Lap 203: Gordon takes the white flag, but it ain't over just yet.

Checkered flag: Now it's over—Gordon, Busch, and Dale Jr. finish 1-2-3.

Four lead changes in the last nine laps make this the wildest, woolliest finish in the Great American Race's dazzling history.

"There are races that you don't want to end, like last November," explained Gordon later, referring to his having run out of catch-up time in the 2004 championship. "Then there are races that can't end fast enough, like this one. You know those guys are gaining on you, but you can't look back or it'll slow you down."

A PROMISE FULFILLED

As Jeff Gordon ran the media gauntlet following the 2005 Daytona 500, he caught himself thinking about the world in which he lived and raced.

"Everything has changed so much," said the 33-year-old superstar, just beginning the 13th season of his Cup career. Then the guy they used to call The Kid laughed. "I used to be the young guy, remember that?"

Sure we do.

When Gordon made his first start, he was a 21-year-old nobody with a mullet cut and a bad mustache. That day in Atlanta, in 1992, he was the youngest racer in the field by seven years and one of only five drivers age 30 or younger. In this day's race, there had been 17 twentysomethings.

Seventeen multimillionaires, each arriving on his private plane, sleeping in his $100,000 motor coach, living life supported by an army of mechanics, marketers, business managers, and Hollywood ca__ from every point on the compass and from every discipline of motorsports: sprint cars, motorcycles, even Formula One.

Smiling, Gordon paused to reflect on the hammer-down world that he, one of the latest in a line of NASCAR titans, had helped build.

From Lee to Richard to Dale and now to Jeff, Bill France's promise had been fulfilled.

The promise that kept fans coming back, kept cars on the racetrack, and kept pedals to the metal.

The promise of what could happen during the next race, the next lap.

The promise that maybe, just maybe, you might witness the next defining NASCAR moment.

INDEX

ACKNOWLEDGMENTS

The acknowledgments page has always been a curious and intimidating concept to me. How does one thank everyone who contributed to his first book? Do I reach all the way back to my second-grade teacher, Mrs. Elliott, for teaching me how to make books with construction paper? Do I keep moving up the ladder to Sory Bowers, Curry Leslie, and Dot Bishop? Oh well, I guess I just did.

So now let me offer my sincere thanks to some folks who have provided much more recent help, counsel, and support.

To the folks at ESPN Books, especially the fearsome fivesome of Chris Raymond, Glen Waggoner, John Glenn, Linda Ng, and the right honorable Mr. Michael Woods. My natural ability to stretch a deadline stretched their collective patience, but friendships forged through phone calls and e-mails turned what can be a painful process into nothing less than a good time. My job was easy. Theirs is what produced the beautiful book you now hold in your hands.

To my friends and colleagues at *ESPN The Magazine*, whose faith in my motorsports knowledge has survived for nearly a decade. J.B. Morris managed to turn a television producer into a writer, with the help of Neil Fine, Gary Belsky, and the countless others who toil at *The Mag's* headquarters in the shadow of the Empire State Building. And to the since-departed Dan Weinberg of ESPN Original Entertainment, who called on an old screening room friend for help with The Worldwide Leader's reentry into NASCAR.

To Stu Hothem at FoxSports.com, who has long given me way too much creative license. To Jud Laghi at LJK for hunting the white whale, and to Richard Ben Cramer for reminding me that I am indeed a writer during a time when others wanted me to believe otherwise. To my TV bosses, from Barry Sacks to Patti Wheeler to Jay Abraham, who have supported and encouraged my sportswriter alter ego in the midst of my day jobs.

Since 1996, my NASCAR mentor has been no less than the greatest stock car writer who ever walked the face of this planet: Tom "Pappy" Higgins of *The Charlotte Observer* and various other parts unknown. God help us all if he ever decides to publish the "real" history of the sport. Along with Greg Fielden and Peter Golenbock, Pap has refused to let NASCAR's colorful past fall prey to the sport's historical revisionists.

To the McGee clan of the Old North State, from the family's first author, father Jerry, to its next, brother Sam. Everything we accomplish is done in memory of my mother, Hannah, and in honor of my grandparents. While so many families were busy preaching about the dangers of dreaming, mine always challenged me to spend every day as creatively as I could.

Finally, to the girls at home: daughter Tara, who so far loves NASCAR only because it makes cool noises, and my wife, Erica, forever the noncredited editor, forced to read or listen to the original versions of anything I write, then refusing to let it leave the house that way. Come to think of it, you should all be thanking her…

—JRM
December 2006

CREDITS

Endpapers: © David Allio; p. 5: Dargan Watts Collection; pp. 6–7 (all): International Motorsports Hall of Fame; pp. 8–9 (all): CIA Stock Photo

'30s, '40s & '50s

p. 10: Jack Cansler/International Motorsports Hall of Fame; pp. 11–12: International Motorsports Hall of Fame; pp. 14–15: Motorsports Images & Archives used with permission; p. 18: International Motorsports Hall of Fame; p. 19: Motorsports Images & Archives used with permission; p. 20: International Motorsports Hall of Fame; p. 22: International Motorsports Hall of Fame; p. 23: Motorsports Images & Archives used with permission; p. 24: Russ Reed/West Coast Stock Car Hall of Fame Collection; pp. 26–27: Dargan Watts Collection; p. 28: Motorsports Nichels Engineering Archives, pp. 30–31: Motorsports Images & Archives used with permission; p. 32: Dargan Watts Collection; p. 33: International Motorsports Hall of Fame; pp. 34–35 (all): Motorsports Images & Archives used with permission; p. 35 (tickets): Dargan Watts Collection; p. 36: International Motorsports Hall of Fame; p. 37: International Motorsports Hall of Fame

'60s

pp. 38–39: International Motorsports Hall of Fame; p. 44: International Motorsports Hall of Fame; p. 45: International Motorsports Hall of Fame; pp. 46–47: AP Photo/Jack Renn; pp. 48–49: Motorsports Images & Archives used with permission; p. 50: www.JoeWeatherly.com; p. 51: BC; pp. 54–55: International Motorsports Hall of Fame; pp. 56–57: Skeet McKinnon/Dargan Watts Collection; pp. 58–59: courtesy of www.curtisturnermuseum.com; p. 61: AP Photo; pp. 62–63: Norman Poole; p. 65: National Motor Museum, Beaulieu; p. 66: Norman Poole; pp. 68–69: Don Hunter Photography; pp. 70–73: International Motorsports Hall of Fame

'70s

pp. 74–75: © Bettmann/CORBIS; pp. 80–81: Motorsports Images & Archives used with permission; p. 82: International Motorsports Hall of Fame; p. 85: International Motor of Motor Racing; p. 87: Jim Nise/Eastern Museum of Motor Racing; p. 88: Dozier Mobley Archives; pp. 90–91: Motorsports Images & Archives used with permission; pp. 92–93: Motorsports Images & Archives used with permission; pp. 94–95: © Bettmann/CORBIS; pp. 96–97: Motorsports Images & Archives used with permission; pp. 100–p. 98: International Historical Racing Moments, LLC; p. 102 101: © Chobat's Historical Racing Moments, LLC; p. 102 (crash photo): AP Photo; pp. 102–103 (fight photos): AP Photo/Ric Feld; p. 104 (all): International Motorsports Hall of Fame; p. 105: © David Allio; pp. 106–107: Motorsports Images & Archives used with permission; p. 109: International Motorsports Hall of Fame

'80s

pp. 110–111: Motorsports Images & Archives used with permission; p. 114: Dozier Mobley Archives; pp. 116–117: AP Photo/Reed Saxon; pp. 118–119: © Chobat's Historical Racing Moments, LLC; p. 121: International Motorsports Hall of Fame; pp. 122—123 (all): Motorsports Images & Archives used with permission; p. 124: © Chobat's Historical Racing Moments,LLC; p. 125: Jerry Wachter/Sports Illustrated; p. 126: © Bettmann/CORBIS; pp. 128–129: James Crabtree/TheInsideGroove.com; pp. 132–133: Daytona Beach News-Journal; p. 135: Dozier Mobley Archives; p. 138: AP Photo/Joanna Pinneo; p. 140: Motorsports Images & Archives used with permission; p. 143: Motorsports Images & Archives used with permission; pp. 144–145: courtesy of Lowe's Motor Speedway; p. 146: © Chobat's Historical Racing Moments, LLC; pp. 148–149: Motorsports Images & Archives used with permission; pp. 150–151: © David Allio; p. 153: AP Photo/Doug Jennings; pp. 154–155: Dozier Mobley Archives; pp. 156–157: Mark and Shannon Weaver; pp. 158–159 (all): Dozier Mobley Archives

'90s

pp. 160–161: © Chobat's Historical Racing Moments, LLC; pp. 164–165: CIA Stock Photo; pp. 166–167: Dozier Mobley Archives; pp. 168–169 (all): © David Allio; p. 172–173: courtesy of Jarrett Family Collection; pp. 174–171: © Chobat's Historical Racing Moments & Archives used with 175 (all): Motorsports Images & Archives used with permission; pp. 176–177: International Motorsports Hall of Fame; p. 178: Dozier Mobley Archives; p. 181: AP Photo/Terry Renna; p. 184: Motorsports Images & Archives used with permission; p. 186: Don Kelly Photo; pp. 188–189: © Chobat's Historical Racing Moments, LLC; p. 190: © Kevin Fleming/CORBIS; p. 191: AP Photo/Bill Sikes; pp. 192–193: Motorsports Images & Archives used with permission; pp. 194–195: © David Allio; pp. 196–197: Motorsports Images & Archives used with permission; pp. 198–199: © Chobat's Historical Racing Moments, LLC; p. 201: Motorsports Images & Archives used with permission

'00s

pp. 204–205: © George Tiedemann/GT Images/Corbis; p. 208: AP Photo/Jaime Dispenza/News and Record; p. 209: Motorsports Images & Archives used with permission; p. 211: International Motorsports Hall of Fame; pp. 214–215: Ray Rosato/Sports Illustrated; pp. 216–217: Phelen Ebenhack/Orlando 213: Bob Sentinel July 9, 2001; p. 218: © Reuters/CORBIS; p. 219: Jim McIsaac/Getty Images; p. 221: AP Photo/Chris O'Meara; p. 224: AP Photo/AP Photo/Chuck Burton; p. 226: © STRINGER/USA/Reuters/Corbis; p. 227: © Sam Sharpe/The Sharpe Image/Corbis; pp. 222–223: Don Kelly Photo; pp. 228–229: CIA Stock Photo; pp. 232–233: Darrell Ingham/Getty Images; p. 234: CIA Stock Photo; pp. 236–237 (clockwise from top left): © George Tiedemann/NewSport/Corbis, AP Photo/Ashley Fleming, Winston Luzier, © Reuters/CORBIS, AP Photo/Pryor, AP Photo/Rusty Kennedy, Don Kelly Photo, AP Photo/David Graham, © Bettmann/CORBIS

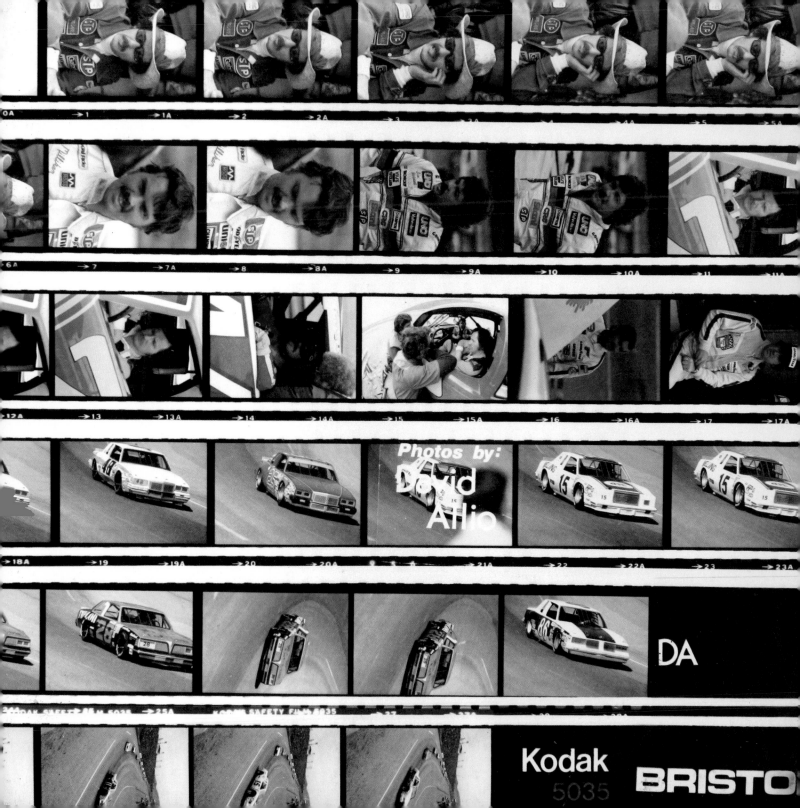